DEDICATION

To all parents, because you have decided to take on *the* most challenging job- to knowingly or unknowingly become role models for your children.

Special thanks go to my parents, Eduardo and Graciela, whose unwavering love and guidance shaped who I am today. Your wisdom and support have always been a light in my life. Even in times of darkness, you both kept being there for me with love and support.

To my beloved spouse, Conor, your role in this rollercoaster ride of parenting is invaluable. Thank you for your patience, encouragement, and for walking beside me every step of the way. You make everything possible.

To my brother, Eduardo, you know how much you helped me get through my dark night of the soul.

And to my children, William, Emily, and James, whose laughter and joy inspire me every day, thank you for filling my world with love and purpose and pushing me to become an even better mom and human being. Your presence in my life has been a source of immense personal growth and I am forever grateful for that.

This book is a testament to the love and strength you've all given me, which has been the cornerstone of my life and the inspiration behind my work.

CONTENTS

INTRODUCTION

"The wound is the place where the Light enters you". Rumi

The memory is burned into my mind, impossible to forget. I see myself standing in the kitchen, frozen, as my two-year-old son accidentally knocks over a glass of milk. A simple spill—something any parent might sigh about or even laugh off. But what happens next is anything but trivial.

I explode. My voice, loud and sharp, slices through the air. I scream at my child's frightened face, rage surging through me like an uncontrollable force. My hands tremble. My heart races. And as the last echoes of my outburst fade, shame and regret settle in their place.

This isn't new. This anger is familiar—too familiar. It follows me like a shadow, a ghost from my past that I can't seem to shake. Standing there in that kitchen, I realize the truth: I am reliving the very patterns I swore I would break. The wounds of my inner child—the ones I thought I had left behind—are demanding my attention. They are screaming to be healed.

In that moment, I know that healing is not just an abstract concept—it is a necessity for me to stop reacting.

For years, I carried my childhood pain without realizing how deeply it shaped me. I didn't see how it controlled my reactions, my emotions, my relationships. But that moment with my son changed everything. It forced me to confront what I had ignored for too long. It showed me that unless I healed, I would continue to pass down the very pain I once endured.

I know I'm not alone in this.

Maybe you, too, have felt triggered in ways you can't explain. Maybe your reactions surprise or scare you, leaving you wondering where all that emotion is coming from. Maybe you find yourself struggling with self-doubt, trust issues, or patterns of self-sabotage that keep holding you back.

This is the legacy of an unhealed inner child.

A wounded inner child shows up in adulthood as low self-worth, difficulty regulating emotions, perfectionism, fear of abandonment, people-pleasing, trust issues, addiction, boundary struggles, and self-sabotage. What many people don't realize is that these wounds don't just stay buried inside us—they influence every aspect of our lives.

That is why I wrote this book.

This is a guide to inner child healing—helping you nurture self-love, build trust, and break free from the patterns that no longer serve you. Through practical strategies, psychological insights, and healing exercises, you'll embark on a journey of self-discovery and emotional freedom.

Inside these pages, you will find:

- Practical strategies to heal your inner child

- Tools to overcome self-sabotage, trust issues, and emotional blocks

- Ways to create healthier relationships—with yourself and others

- A roadmap to cultivating resilience, self-compassion, and emotional balance

Because unhealed childhood wounds often show up in parenting, I have also included a special chapter on how inner child healing connects to breaking generational cycles. This chapter will help you recognize how your past influences the way you parent (or how you see your own caregivers) and offer tools to stop passing down pain unconsciously. Even if you aren't a parent, this chapter will allow you to view your upbringing with more clarity and compassion, helping you shift your perspective on those who hurt you.

This book is grounded in both personal experience and the latest psychological research. It weaves together personal stories, case studies, and science-backed healing techniques to guide you toward transformation. Each chapter is designed to help you take meaningful steps toward self-awareness, emotional resilience, and lasting change.

Let me introduce myself. My name is Michelle Duffy, and I am a transformational teacher and empowerment coach for women. My healing journey began over a decade ago, triggered by my own childhood trauma, the struggles of early motherhood, and a near-death experience during childbirth. Through my work—both personal and professional—I have discovered powerful tools for healing, and I have had the privilege of guiding countless others on their own journeys.

I know what it feels like to carry pain that was never yours to hold. I also know that healing is possible.

This book is your companion on the path to wholeness. It will walk with you as you uncover your wounds, face them with compassion, and release their hold on you. Healing requires courage, but you don't have to do it alone.

I invite you to begin this journey with me.

Let's heal together.

CHAPTER ONE

UNDERSTANDING YOUR INNER CHILD

"When we honor our inner child's feelings, we release the emotional hurts that we're still subconsciously carrying around." Patricia Hope

Have you ever found yourself reacting to a situation with an intensity that seemed disproportionate to the event? Perhaps a disagreement with a friend or a critical comment at work left you feeling unexpectedly hurt or angry. If this resonates with you, you are not alone. These moments often stem from the unhealed parts of our past, the echoes of our inner child seeking to be heard and understood. Recognizing and connecting with this part of ourselves is the first step in breaking free from these patterns and moving toward healing.

Who Is Your Inner Child?

The inner child is a metaphorical concept representing the childlike aspect within each of us. It embodies the early emotional experiences that have shaped us, both the joyful and the painful. This part of ourselves holds our younger years' vulnerability, creativity, and innocence. Despite its abstract nature, the inner child has profound significance in our psychological and emotional development. It influences our behaviors, decision-making, and emotional responses in ways we might not even realize. Recognizing this influence allows us to understand why we react the way we do and begin to change those reactions for the better.

The concept of the inner child finds its roots in Carl Jung's work, where he explored the idea of the child archetype as a crucial part of the human psyche. Jung's theories have since been expanded in various therapeutic practices, emphasizing the importance of reconnecting with this inner aspect.

Modern psychological approaches, such as Neuro-Linguistic Programming (NLP), suggest that our subconscious mind, where the inner child resides, governs much of our adult behavior. Neuroscience tells us that children before age eight are *exclusively* in their subconscious mind; the conscious mind develops after that age. The NLP research proposes that only having the subconscious mind allows children to absorb everything, like sponges, and form the beliefs that will be used later in life. It's as if the child's mind is writing the programming of how a relationship should look, how to talk about money, what is right and wrong, etc., all coming from the authoritative figures in their life.

Our inner child *significantly* impacts our relationships and self-esteem. It can influence how we connect with others, perceive ourselves, and respond to life's challenges. If the inner child feels neglected or wounded, it can manifest as trust issues, self-doubt, or a tendency toward self-sabotage. Acknowledging and nurturing this part of ourselves is crucial for personal growth and development. This is what's known as **reparenting** and it can transform these patterns into healthier, more constructive ways of being.

Engaging with the inner child is important because it has the potential for holistic healing. When we acknowledge and reconnect with this part of ourselves, we open the door to emotional healing and behavioral change. This process not only alleviates the emotional pain we carry but also empowers us to move forward with greater clarity and purpose. Through this work, we learn to respond to life's challenges with resilience and understanding, fostering a sense of inner peace and balance.

Recognizing Childhood Wounds

Understanding the nuances of childhood wounds begins with identifying the core emotional scars that continue to affect us. These wounds often stem from experiences such as feeling abandoned, rejected, or criticized during formative years. Common wounds include feelings of inadequacy, betrayal, and loss. They are often deeply embedded in our subconscious, shaping our perceptions and interactions. The symptoms of unresolved trauma can manifest subtly yet pervasively in adulthood. You may experience difficulty trusting others, chronic anxiety, or an inexplicable sense of sadness. These are echoes of the past, reminders of what the inner child endured but could not process at the time. Recognizing these signs allows us to acknowledge the pain and begin addressing it.

Repressed memories often linger beneath the surface, influencing our adult lives unexpectedly. Emotional flashbacks are one of the primary manifestations of these hidden memories. You might overreact to seemingly benign situations, only to realize that the emotional response is rooted in a forgotten experience. Unexplained anxiety or depression can also be indicators of repressed memories trying to surface. These feelings often arise without an apparent cause, leaving you puzzled and overwhelmed. Recognizing these signs can be challenging, but it's crucial for understanding the depth of your wounds. Acknowledging these feelings allows you to explore their origins with compassion and curiosity, paving the way for healing and growth.

Even overachievement, workaholism, and perfectionism may stem from childhood wounds, where children are validated *exclusively* for their achievements rather than for being themselves. To keep feeling accepted and loved, adults do everything possible to achieve more.

The role of caregivers in shaping childhood wounds cannot be overstated. Parents and caregivers wield *immense* influence over a child's emotional development. **Neglect** and **criticism** can inflict deep wounds that persist into adulthood, fostering feelings of unworthiness and self-doubt. Similarly, **shame** can erode a child's sense of self, leaving them with a lingering belief in their inadequacy. While often well-intentioned, overprotectiveness can also contribute to childhood wounds by stifling a child's ability to explore and assert their independence. This dynamic can lead to challenges in developing autonomy and confidence in adulthood. Understanding these interactions helps us recognize how our early environment shaped our emotional landscape. <u>It also allows us to approach these wounds with empathy rather than blame, acknowledging that our caregivers often did their best with what they knew.</u>

The legacy of childhood experiences extends far beyond the early years, creating patterns that perpetuate into adulthood. These experiences often lay the foundation for recurring relationship issues, where unresolved emotional scars manifest as difficulties in building trust or maintaining healthy boundaries. Patterns of self-sabotage, such as procrastination or persistent self-doubt, are also common byproducts of unhealed childhood wounds. These behaviors can hinder personal and professional growth, trapping us in cycles of frustration and disappointment. Recognizing these patterns enables us to take proactive steps toward change. By understanding the origins of our behaviors, we can rewrite the narratives that have held us back, fostering a sense of empowerment and control over our lives.

Childhood Trauma and Its Impact on Adulthood

Childhood trauma is a profound experience that leaves an indelible mark on our lives. It encompasses a range of experiences, from emotional abuse to physical neglect, that disrupt a child's sense of safety and security. As Dr. Peter Levine describes, trauma is "a *perceived* threat and the inability to respond." This definition captures the essence of trauma—a moment where a child feels overwhelmed and powerless, unable to process the intensity of their emotions. Trauma originates from *perceived* threats and thus, to varying extents, affects everyone. It can range from minor incidents, such as the fear instilled by a kitten's scratch or the threat of missing a cherished social event as a form of punishment, to the more profound and widely acknowledged traumas resulting from experiences of assault or exposure to war.

Emotional abuse, for example, chips away at a child's self-worth through constant criticism or belittlement, leaving scars that persist into adulthood. Physical neglect, on the other hand, deprives a child of basic needs, fostering feelings of abandonment and unworthiness. These early experiences can set the stage for a lifetime of challenges as the child grows into an adult burdened by unresolved pain.

The impact of childhood trauma extends far beyond the early years, manifesting in various psychological effects as we mature. Chronic anxiety is one such consequence, often rooted in the hypervigilance developed during traumatic experiences. This constant state of alertness can be exhausting, leading to a pervasive sense of unease that clouds our daily lives. Dysfunctional relationship patterns also emerge as trauma shapes our expectations and interactions with others. We might find ourselves drawn to relationships that mirror the chaos of our past or struggle to trust those who genuinely care for us. These patterns, while challenging to break, are not insurmountable. Understanding their origins is the first step toward healing and creating healthier, more fulfilling connections.

Trauma doesn't only affect the mind; it is deeply embedded in the body as well. The concept of trauma, as somatic, highlights how these experiences are stored physically, manifesting as various symptoms throughout our body. Somatic symptom disorders, for instance, might arise when unresolved trauma expresses itself through unexplained physical ailments. Chronic pain, too, can be a remnant of past trauma, residing in muscles and joints long after the initial event has passed. It's as if the body holds on to the memory of what happened, reminding us in subtle yet persistent ways. Recognizing this connection between mind and body is crucial for holistic healing. By addressing the physical manifestations of trauma, we begin to alleviate the emotional burden that accompanies them.

Despite the deep-seated nature of childhood trauma, there is hope for healing and recovery. Neuroplasticity—the brain's ability to change and adapt—offers a promising path forward. This concept suggests that, with the right support and interventions, we can rewire our brains to overcome the effects of trauma. Therapies like Somatic Experiencing have shown remarkable success in helping individuals process and integrate traumatic memories. These approaches tap into the brain's innate capacity for healing, guiding us toward resilience and strength. Later in this book, you will experience somatic healing through the practice of mindfulness. When combined with inner child healing, this approach is extremely effective for trauma recovery. Stories of recovery from childhood trauma abound, illustrating the transformative power of therapy and personal growth. They remind us that we are not defined by our past, but by our capacity to heal and thrive.

Trauma's Impact on the Brain and Body

When we discuss trauma, we often focus on the emotional scars it leaves behind. However, its impact on the brain and body is both profound and complex. Trauma can alter brain function and structure, manifesting in ways that affect our daily lives. For example, the hippocampus—a region of the brain responsible for memory and learning—can experience reduced activity and size due to prolonged exposure to trauma. This alteration can lead to difficulties in forming new memories or recalling past ones, leaving individuals with gaps in recollection or a distorted sense of time. It's therefore not uncommon to have few memories of your childhood, *especially* if you endured traumatic events.

Moreover, the amygdala, the brain's emotional processing center, becomes hyperactive. It overreacts to **perceived** threats, often triggering a heightened state of alertness or anxiety. This hypervigilance can make even minor stress overwhelming, as if one is constantly walking through life with a sense of looming danger.

According to Peter Levine's research, **repetitive behaviors** often emerge as individuals unconsciously attempt to process and release trauma. These behaviors, while sometimes appearing benign, can become a means of coping with the unresolved trauma embedded within the body. Some examples of these coping mechanisms are compulsive overeating or restrictive eating, excessive exercise, nail biting, procrastination, compulsive cleaning, people pleasing, and substance abuse.

The mind-body connection plays a vital role in understanding how trauma affects us. Our mental processes and physical health are intertwined, influencing each other. Psychosomatic responses—where psychological distress manifests as physical symptoms—highlight this connection. For example, a person experiencing anxiety might also suffer from digestive issues or skin rashes, conditions that are rooted in emotional turmoil rather than physical illness.

Understanding the impact of trauma on the brain and body has significant implications for treatment and recovery. By recognizing that trauma alters brain structure and function, we can develop targeted therapies that focus on brain plasticity. These therapies aim to re-establish equilibrium within the brain, reducing the amygdala's hyperactivity and enhancing the hippocampus's function.

Techniques such as mindfulness, yoga, and somatic experiencing, which focus on the body's physical sensations, work alongside cognitive therapies to address the full spectrum of trauma's effects. This strategy, which encompasses mind and body techniques, is used in this book. This holistic approach not only aims to resolve the physiological and psychological symptoms of trauma but also empowers individuals to reclaim their health and well-being.

Emotional Triggers: Recognize and Respond

Emotional triggers are events that seem harmless at first but suddenly bring up strong emotions, catching us by surprise. These triggers are linked to past experiences, often from childhood, when we felt pain, fear, or anger. They're like old memories that resurface when something similar happens again. For many women, a hurtful comment from a partner or a dismissive tone from a colleague can spark an intense emotional reaction. The strong feelings aren't just about what's happening now—they also bring up unresolved emotions from the past. Recognizing these triggers is an important step in becoming more self-aware and understanding our emotions better.

Attention to your emotional responses in various situations is essential to identifying personal triggers. I always say, "**Awareness** is *the first step* to changing behavior." When you're unaware of what is happening, you will continue getting triggered by the same events and repeating negative cycles. Reflective journaling can be a powerful tool here. In the following chapters, we will review this writing technique in greater detail, but now, I highly recommend that you get a journal *exclusively* for the work you will be doing with healing your inner child.

By writing down the events that provoke strong emotions, you can begin to see patterns emerge. Consider asking yourself:

- "What was I feeling before this incident?"

- "Does this remind me of a past event?"

- "Does this reaction and the words used remind me of someone saying that to me as a child?"

- "Was I worried or stressed about something else?"

We are often not angry about something that just happened but that triggered something already bothering us. An example is when your kid breaks something, and you get outraged, but the anger comes from your current problems at work that keep you stressed out.

The reflective process mentioned above helps map out the *emotional* terrain of your inner world. When you ask yourself a question, the subconscious mind answers. You will get an answer immediately, several hours, or days later (sometimes in the strangest moments, like when you shower). Nonetheless, you *will* always get an answer from your subconscious mind, so keep asking the right questions. What do I mean by the right questions? Most people ask, "Why?" as in, "Why is this happening to me?" But "why" questions don't give you insights; they only produce your negative talk. The best questions are "what," "when," and "how." So, instead of "Why is this happening to me?" which can lead you to "This always happens to me!" or "I'm an idiot" (which is not valid, but are things you heard as a child), the question "What does this story remind me of?" looks for clues to where this originated from.

Another effective exercise is visualizing past events that have left a strong emotional imprint. You can gently revisit these memories to uncover the links between past experiences and current triggers. This practice is about *connecting the dots* and seeing how the past weaves into the present.

Managing emotional triggers is essential for maintaining emotional health. When left unchecked, these triggers can lead to emotional over-whelm, a state where the intensity of feelings becomes too much to handle. This can manifest as anxiety, irritability, or even physical symptoms like headaches or fatigue. Learning to manage triggers enhances emotional resilience, enabling you to navigate life's challenges with grace and confidence. It involves developing a toolkit of strategies to calm the storm before it takes over. By understanding and managing these triggers, you gain control over your emotional responses, fostering a sense of inner peace and balance. This understanding underpins the perspective I share with my clients: "Triggers are hidden treasures." Uncovering these triggers allows you to address and resolve situations with thoughtful responses instead of exacerbating them through reactive behavior.

Practical methods for handling triggers revolve around grounding techniques and mindful breathing exercises (we will review these in greater detail throughout the book). Grounding techniques are about anchoring yourself to the present moment, pulling you away from the emotional turmoil. Simple methods like focusing on the sensation of your feet on the floor or the texture of an object in your hand can break the cycle of emotional escalation. Mindful breathing exercises, on the other hand, involve taking slow, deep breaths to calm the nervous system. By concentrating on the rhythm of your breath, you can create a space of calmness within yourself. These practices allow you to pause and reset, offering a moment of reprieve from the intensity of the trigger. Integrating these techniques into your daily routine can provide a foundation of stability, helping you respond to life's challenges with newfound resilience.

Understanding Emotional Baggage

Emotional baggage is a term that many of us have heard yet might not fully understand. It refers to the unresolved conflicts and regrets we carry from past experiences, often without realizing it. These burdens accumulate over time, layer by layer, as we navigate through life. Each disappointment, unprocessed feeling, or unresolved argument can add to this load, lingering like a shadow. These emotions affect our interactions and how we see the world. Negative feelings such as anger, sadness, or guilt can become ingrained, influencing our perceptions and responses. We might not even know their presence, yet they silently shape our decisions and relationships.

In daily life, emotional baggage can weigh heavily on our mood and outlook. It's like wearing tinted glasses that color everything we see. This weight can lead to a sense of heaviness, impacting how we approach each day. It might cause us to react more strongly to minor frustrations or feel drained without reason. Our careers and personal goals can also suffer, as this baggage often breeds self-doubt and hesitancy. The fear of repeating past mistakes can hold us back from taking risks or pursuing opportunities. Decisions become clouded, and the energy needed to chase our dreams can feel elusive as if we're running a marathon with invisible weights tied to our ankles.

To address and release emotional baggage, we must first acknowledge it. Cognitive behavioral techniques offer practical ways to do this. By identifying and challenging negative thought patterns, we can change our narrative. For instance, reframing a perceived failure as a learning experience can lessen its emotional impact. "Letting go" rituals can also be effective. These rituals might involve writing a letter to someone who hurt you, detailing your feelings, and then disposing of it in a way that symbolizes release. This act can be cathartic, offering a sense of closure even if the person is no longer in your life or alive. Through these processes, we create space for healing and new perspectives. In the following chapters, you will be led to do these exercises using a step-by-step guide.

Releasing this emotional baggage can lead to profound benefits. Imagine the freedom of moving through life without the constant weight of past regrets. Emotional resilience increases as we learn to respond to challenges with clarity and strength. We're better equipped to handle stress and adapt to change, feeling more grounded and centered. Personal relationships also improve. As we let go of the past, we become more open and present, fostering more profound connections. The walls built from past hurts begin to crumble, allowing for genuine intimacy and trust. This openness invites new experiences and growth, enriching our lives unexpectedly.

The Role of Shame and Guilt in Inner Child Wounds

Shame and guilt are emotions that often intertwine, yet they hold distinct places within our psyche. To understand the role of these negative emotions in our lives, it is essential to differentiate between them. Shame is a feeling deeply rooted in one's sense of self; it whispers something inherently wrong with who we are. It suggests a state of being flawed or unworthy, casting shadows over our identity. In contrast, guilt is more about our actions. It arises when we believe we have done something wrong, reflecting on our behaviors rather than our core self. This distinction is crucial, as it shapes how we perceive and respond to these emotions throughout our lives.

In childhood, the seeds of shame and guilt are often sown through parental expectations and societal pressures. When caregivers place unrealistic demands on children or fail to provide unconditional love, it can lead to a pervasive sense of shame. Children may internalize the belief that they are not good enough, carrying this burden into adulthood. Similarly, societal norms and judgments can instill guilt as we strive to meet external standards that may not align with our true selves. These formative experiences imprint on our inner child and influence how we navigate the world.

An example I often see is when parents use labels like "good girl" or "bad girl," which shape a child's identity instead of addressing specific behaviors. If a child does something wrong, it's more helpful to describe it as "bad behavior" because behavior can change, whereas saying "bad girl" suggests something inherently wrong with the child. Unfortunately, many adults grew up hearing these labels, leading to guilt and shame about who they are. There's nothing wrong with us; the words used in our early years left lasting marks, almost like imprints on our skin. Now, it's up to us to recognize that we are not these labels or defined by our behaviors. We can change if we choose to, and by reading this book, that's precisely what you're doing.

Entrenched shame and guilt have detrimental effects on personal growth. They can act as invisible chains, holding us back from reaching our full potential. When these emotions take root, they can lead to self-destructive behaviors, such as self-sabotage or substance abuse. The fear of being exposed or judged can inhibit self-expression, stifling creativity and authenticity. We may find ourselves trapped in a cycle of self-criticism, unable to embrace our true selves. This cycle can be exhausting, eroding self-esteem and hindering our capacity for meaningful connections.

Overcoming these pervasive emotions requires intentional effort and self-compassion. One effective strategy is to cultivate self-compassion practices that foster a kinder relationship with ourselves. This involves treating ourselves with the same empathy and understanding we would offer a dear friend. Acknowledging our humanity and imperfections is a vital step in releasing the grip of shame. Affirmations for self-forgiveness can also be transformative. By regularly reminding ourselves that we are worthy of forgiveness, we can begin to dismantle the walls that shame and guilt have built. These affirmations are powerful tools, helping to rewire our thought patterns and promote healing. You will learn how to craft your affirmations in Chapter Three.

As we address these emotions, we must remember that healing is a process. It takes time and patience to untangle the threads of shame and guilt that have woven their way into our lives. Yet, by embracing self-compassion and forgiveness, we can free our inner child from the constraints of these burdens. This liberation opens the door to self-acceptance, allowing us to step into our power with confidence and grace. With each step forward, we move closer to a life where our past no longer dictates our future and where we can express our true selves without fear.

Chapter Two

THE PATH TO HEALING YOUR INNER CHILD

"Your past does not define you. The healing process does."
Dr. Thema Bryant-Davis

Picture walking into a space where you feel enveloped in warmth and safety, a place where your heart can open and your mind can rest. Creating such a sanctuary is vital for those seeking to heal their inner child, as it provides a foundation of security and calmness essential for delving into deep emotional work. For many women, a safe space extends beyond physical walls; it encompasses a psychological realm where vulnerability is not only allowed but encouraged. Here, you can explore your emotions without fear of judgment or retribution, a crucial step in unraveling the knots of past trauma.

Establishing both physical and emotional safety is a cornerstone of effective healing. Begin by setting up personal retreat spaces in your home—areas that feel sacred and serene. These might be small nooks filled with cherished objects, soft cushions, and gentle lighting. Such environments can serve as havens where you retreat to reflect and process emotions. Equally important is boundary setting with those around you. Communicate your need for uninterrupted time and space clearly, ensuring that others respect your emotional sanctuary. This act of self-care sends a powerful message: Your healing is a priority.

The design of your physical space plays a significant role in fostering a healing environment. Consider the use of calming colors and elements that soothe the senses. Soft blues, gentle greens, and earthy tones can evoke a sense of peace and stability. Incorporate elements of nature, such as plants or natural light, to create a connection with the world outside. The presence of these elements can enhance your sense of well-being, grounding you in the present moment. This thoughtful curation of your surroundings reflects your commitment to nurturing your inner landscape.

Integrating healing practices into your environment can further support your emotional exploration. Create meditation corners where you can sit quietly and connect with your breath, allowing thoughts and feelings to surface gently. Aromatherapy and essential oils can also be supportive, with scents like lavender or chamomile promoting relaxation and calm. These practices help create an atmosphere conducive to introspection, where the focus is on inner peace and self-discovery.

Expressing emotions safely is an integral part of the healing process. Introduce tools and mediums that allow you to explore feelings creatively. Art supplies like paints, pencils, or clay can provide a nonverbal outlet for difficult-to-articulate emotions. Music and movement offer another avenue for expression, where the body becomes a vessel for releasing pent-up energy and emotion. These creative outlets are not just about producing something tangible; they are about the process of expression, a journey into the heart of your emotional world.

Managing intense emotions is a challenge many women face, particularly when delving into the depths of past trauma. Grounding exercises can be invaluable, providing techniques to anchor yourself in the here and now. Simple practices such as focusing on your breath or feeling the weight of your body against the earth can help stabilize your emotional state. Support networks and resources, such as therapy groups or trusted friends, offer *additional* layers of safety, reminding you that you are not alone in this process.

Reflective Exercise: Creating Your Safe Space

Objective: Establish a personal sanctuary for emotional exploration.
Instructions:

1. **Identify a space**. Choose a quiet corner of your home dedicated to healing work.

2. **Personalize.** Gather items that bring you comfort—blankets, photos, meaningful objects.

3. **Incorporate nature.** Add a plant or a minor water feature for a touch of tranquility.

4. **Set boundaries.** Communicate with household members about the importance of this space.

Reflect on how this environment makes you feel. Is there a sense of peace or calmness? Adjust as needed to enhance your comfort.

Building a Relationship With Your Inner Child

The nurturing relationship you build with your inner child is at the heart of healing. This connection is not a destination but a process that requires attention and care. Your inner child, echoing your past, often holds unmet needs. Recognizing these needs is the first step in fostering a relationship based on trust and safety. It's about acknowledging the fears and desires that linger from your younger years, giving them a voice in your present life. When you create a space where your inner child feels safe and heard, you begin to heal the wounds that have been carried for so long. This is what's called "re-parenting," or giving yourself the emotional support and guidance that wasn't given in your childhood. This relationship with your inner child is a sanctuary where your *authentic* self can emerge without fear of judgment or rejection.

Techniques to deepen this bond can be both simple and significant. Visualization exercises allow you to picture and interact with your inner child meaningfully. Imagine a safe, comforting environment where you meet your inner child, offering them love and understanding. These visualizations can be incredibly healing, bridging past and present. Rituals and affirmations also play a vital role. Think about starting each day with a ritual that honors your inner child, such as lighting a candle or speaking words reinforcing love and acceptance. These practices remind your inner child that they are valued and cherished, helping to solidify the bond you are building.

Listening to your inner child requires an openness to subtle and overt expressions. Active listening techniques are crucial here. When you sense a disproportionate emotional response, pause and ask yourself what your inner child might be trying to communicate. This practice involves tuning into the emotions that arise, whether they manifest as anxiety, joy, or sadness. Validate these emotions by acknowledging their presence and importance. This validation is not about solving problems but recognizing and holding space for your inner child's experiences. It means saying, "I hear you, and your voice and feelings matter."

Building this relationship is challenging, and patience is your ally. There will be setbacks, moments when old patterns resurface, or when progress feels stalled. These setbacks are natural and do not erase the work you have done. It is essential to approach these moments with *compassion* rather than frustration. Celebrate small victories along the way, as they are the building blocks of lasting change. Each time you kindly respond to your inner child, you strengthen the foundation of trust and understanding. In this dance of healing, patience, and perseverance guiding you forward, you create a story of resilience and hope.

Introducing Inner Child Dialogue

Engaging in dialogue with your inner child is a therapeutic practice that allows you to address childhood wounds with compassion and understanding. This dialogue is like opening a gentle conversation with a part of yourself that has long been silent, waiting for the right moment to speak. It connects your past to the present, offering insights into behaviors and feelings that might remain hidden. The core purpose of inner child dialogue is to heal those deep-seated emotional wounds that often manifest as unhelpful patterns in adulthood. By speaking with your inner child, you can reframe past experiences to foster healing and growth. The therapeutic benefits of this practice are immense, providing clarity and emotional release and fostering a sense of wholeness. As you engage in this dialogue, you may uncover forgotten memories, gaining a richer understanding of how they shaped who you are today.

Reflect on employing techniques that encourage open communication to initiate and sustain meaningful dialogue with your inner child. One effective method is letter-writing exercises.

Interactive Exercise: Letter Writing Technique

For this exercise, you will need your journal and, if possible, a photograph of yourself (preferably taken between two and eight years old).

Initiate a heartfelt dialogue by composing a letter to your inner child, where you convey deep empathy and understanding for what she's endured. This powerful exercise allows you to express those complex emotions that have remained unspoken or misunderstood for years. By carefully choosing words that resonate with kindness and compassion, you articulate a narrative that acknowledges and validates the experiences of your inner child. This letter becomes a powerful tool for bridging the gap between past hurts and present healing, allowing you to gently confront and soothe the wounds that have lingered in silence. Don't hold back on anything that validates and empowers that child version of you.

You can keep this letter and read it whenever you have doubts, fear, or anxiety. This letter speaks truth as you know yourself more than anyone else, and you're giving yourself the words, love, and encouragement you might not have received when you most needed it.

However, you might face resistance when engaging with your inner child. This resistance often stems from fear of emotional overwhelm or skepticism about the process's validity. It's not uncommon to worry that opening these doors might release feelings too intense to handle. You may also question whether this dialogue can genuinely make a difference. Acknowledge these fears as they arise, but don't let them deter you. Remember that healing is a personal journey, and skepticism is a part of that process. Approach this practice with curiosity and patience, allowing yourself to explore these emotions without judgment. Recognizing and addressing these fears paves the way for a more genuine connection with your inner child, ultimately leading to more profound healing.

Building consistency in your practice of inner child dialogue is crucial for lasting change. You can set aside regular weekly time to engage in this dialogue, treating it as a sacred routine. Consistency reinforces the bond between you and your inner child, demonstrating a commitment to their healing. Each session you can delve deeper into your inner child's needs and emotions. Your writing can range from exploring specific memories to reflecting on current challenges. As you integrate this practice into your daily life, you'll find that the connection with your inner child strengthens, providing insights and understanding that enhance your overall well-being.

The Role of Forgiveness in Healing

Forgiveness is often misunderstood. It's not always about reconciliation or mending broken relationships. Instead, forgiveness is a personal journey toward releasing the heavy burdens of resentment and anger that weigh on *your* soul. It's a conscious decision to let go of the past, not for the sake of others but for your peace and liberation. Many myths surround forgiveness, suggesting it means excusing behavior or forgetting the pain caused. But true forgiveness does not demand forgetting or condoning; it allows you to disentangle your emotions from past hurts, freeing your heart from the shackles of bitterness. This process opens the door to healing, enabling you to move forward with emotional clarity and lightness.

The path to forgiveness begins with yourself. Self-forgiveness is the most challenging yet rewarding aspect of this process. It involves acknowledging your own mistakes and imperfections without harsh self-judgment. Start by reflecting on when you've felt guilt or shame, and write a letter to yourself. This exercise can be cathartic, allowing you to confront your feelings openly and offer yourself the compassion you deserve.

Similarly, guided meditations can facilitate a deeper connection, helping you visualize your inner child in a safe and nurturing environment for forgiveness to occur. As a child, there were many instances when you probably thought that what was happening was all your fault. This is because adults often don't believe children will understand what is happening. Unfortunately, the child's brain not having a reason why things are happening assumes the position of "it has to do with me." This is simply not true, but it's how our brains are wired to work.

During these meditations, envision yourself sitting with your inner child, offering reassurance and love. These practices create a sacred space where your inner child feels acknowledged and valued. By incorporating these techniques, you establish a channel through which your inner child can communicate freely, leading to extensive healing and transformation. To support you further, I've included a free forgiveness meditation for your inner child that you can access via the QR code.

Or go to the website: https://www.michelleduffy1111.com/audiosf orhealingyourinnerchildbook

This meditation is designed to help you connect with your inner child and nurture a forgiving heart. It provides a gentle guide along this path.

Similarly, forgiving others can be facilitated through letters of release. Write to those who have caused you pain, expressing your emotions and intention to let go, even if you never send it. This act of articulation can unburden your spirit, creating space for healing.

Despite the benefits, forgiveness is a challenging road. Resentment and grudges can be formidable barriers, often rooted in the fear of vulnerability. Letting go of these defenses can feel like exposing yourself to more hurt. Resisting this vulnerability is natural, but holding on to pain only prolongs suffering. To overcome these barriers, begin by acknowledging your feelings without judgment. Understand that resentment is a protective mechanism, shielding you from further pain. However, it's also a prison that prevents you from experiencing true freedom and joy. Embrace vulnerability as a strength, not a weakness, and take small steps toward opening your heart.

When you choose to forgive, you embark on a transformative healing process that touches *every* aspect of your life. Forgiveness facilitates emotional liberation, breaking the chains of past grievances that have held you captive. It offers closure, allowing you to find peace in situations that once caused turmoil. This newfound freedom brings a sense of balance and harmony, enabling you to cultivate healthier relationships and a deeper connection with yourself. Forgiving releases the emotional energy tied to past wounds, redirecting it toward growth and self-discovery. As you let go, you create room for love, compassion, and understanding to flourish.

Cognitive Behavioral Techniques for Healing

Cognitive behavioral therapy, or CBT, offers a structured approach to healing that focuses on altering negative thought patterns and enhancing emotional regulation. At its core, CBT is about recognizing the thoughts and beliefs that drive your emotional and behavioral responses. Often, these thoughts are automatic and deeply ingrained, shaped by past experiences, including those from childhood. By shining a light on these patterns, CBT empowers you to challenge and change them, fostering a more balanced emotional state. This process is particularly relevant to inner child work, as it provides a framework for understanding how early experiences continue to influence your present life. Through CBT, you learn to *identify* the distortions in your thinking that contribute to emotional distress, creating space for healing and growth.

To integrate CBT into your daily life, identify and challenge cognitive distortions. These distortions are the exaggerated or irrational thought patterns that fuel negative emotions. For example, you might engage in "all-or-nothing" thinking, where a minor setback feels like a total failure. Start by recognizing these thoughts as they arise and questioning their validity. Ask yourself, "Is this thought based on facts or distorted?" Doing so can reframe your perspective and reduce the *intensity* of your emotional reactions. Another practical tool is using thought records to track your progress. Thought records are journals where you document situations that trigger emotional responses, along with your thoughts and feelings. Over time, this practice helps you identify recurring patterns and develop strategies to manage them more effectively.

CBT also includes exercises specifically designed to build emotional resilience. One such exercise involves **reframing** negative beliefs about self-worth. Often, these beliefs are rooted in childhood experiences, where messages about your values are internalized. To reframe these beliefs, start by identifying the core belief and writing it down. Then, ask yourself if this is true or just a story you've been telling yourself. Finally, challenge it by listing evidence that contradicts it. For example, if you believe "I'm not good enough," write down instances where you demonstrated competence and strength. This exercise helps shift your mindset, replacing negative with more balanced, positive beliefs. Developing problem-solving skills is another crucial aspect of CBT. By breaking down challenges into manageable steps, you can approach problems with clarity and confidence, reducing feelings of overwhelm and helplessness.

Examples of limiting core beliefs most people have and that you want to explore in your writing:

- "I'm not good enough." (This can be "I'm not smart, pretty, slim, eloquent, etc. enough.")

- "I'm not worthy." (This equates to not feeling significant or not deserving happiness or fulfillment.)

Write down why these beliefs are false and all the evidence that you are good enough and worthy of happiness and fulfillment.

The benefits of CBT in inner child healing are far-reaching. By improving **self-awareness**, CBT enables you to gain insight into the origins of your emotional responses, fostering clarity and understanding.

This heightened awareness allows you to recognize patterns that no longer serve you and take steps to change them. CBT also enhances coping strategies for stress, equipping you with tools to navigate life's challenges with resilience. You may notice a shift in your emotional landscape as you practice these techniques. Feelings of anxiety and sadness become less overwhelming, replaced by a sense of empowerment and control. The skills you develop through CBT aid in healing childhood wounds and lay the foundation for a more fulfilling and harmonious life.

Somatic Practices for Releasing Childhood Trauma

In the realm of healing, somatic practices offer a deep approach to releasing trauma that has embedded itself within the body. These therapies recognize that trauma is not just a mental experience but also a physical one stored within our muscles, tissues, and nervous systems. Body-focused psychotherapy and somatic experiencing are two methods that delve into this connection, providing a pathway to release what has been held for too long. Somatic Experiencing, developed by Dr. Peter Levine, focuses on the idea that trauma can be trapped in the body, causing tension and stress. By gently guiding individuals through bodily sensations, this approach helps to discharge the energy associated with traumatic memories, promoting healing and balance.

Effective somatic techniques vary, yet all aim to reconnect the mind and body in a harmonious dance.

Interactive Exercise: Progressive Muscle Relaxation Technique

(a practice where you systematically tense and relax different muscle groups)

Objective: Alleviate physical tension in the body from stress, promote relaxation, and enhance body awareness.

Instructions:

1. **Find a quiet space**. You can lie down on your back, or you can even do this before you get out of bed in the morning.

2. **Get comfortable**. Feel your body relax and close your eyes if that feels comfortable to you.

3. **Focus on your body.** Bring attention to your body as you're breathing.

4. **Tense your body**. Tense *every* part of your body, including your face, for 5–10 seconds.

5. **Release**. Then, let every muscle relax with a loud sigh of relief. Do this two or three times, bringing awareness to the parts of your body that are tight or in pain.

This action alleviates physical tension and fosters an understanding of where stress resides within your body.

Interactive Exercise: Tension and Trauma Release Exercises (TRE)

Objective: Help the body shake off accumulated stress.

Instructions:

1. Find a safe space to do your movements. Use a yoga mat or blanket.

2. Lay down facing up with your legs bent and feet resting on the floor. Start with deep, mindful breaths, placing one hand in your stomach and another on your heart space.

3. Initiate the tremor response. You can do this in several ways: lift your heels and hips off the ground a couple of inches and notice how your body starts to have involuntary tremors from the fatigue. Observe the sensation and breathe slowly and mindfully through the shaking. This can last from a few seconds to a couple of minutes. Another position for activating the tremors is to sway your legs side to side in that same laying-down position. Other positions are standing up, like putting your back to a wall and sliding down as if it seems like you're sitting in a chair. Holding that position will bring about involuntary tremors.

4. Release and rest. After a couple of rounds of this, just rest and let the tremors subside. Take a moment to do a quick body scan and see how your body is feeling.

5. Reflect. Take a moment to write about the experience and any sensations or feelings.

These exercises mimic animals' natural processes to return to calm after a stressful encounter. Embodied movement practices, like mindful dance or yoga, further facilitate this release, encouraging you to move with intention and awareness. These techniques invite you to listen to your body's wisdom, allowing it to guide you toward healing.

The benefits of engaging with somatic practices are both lasting and transformative. As you tune into your body's signals, you begin to process and release trauma in a way that words alone cannot achieve. Emotional regulation becomes more accessible as you learn to recognize and modulate the physical sensations associated with emotional distress. This increased bodily awareness fosters a sense of presence and grounding, enabling you to navigate life's challenges more easily. You develop a deeper understanding of your physical and emotional self through somatic work, cultivating a compassionate relationship with your body. This connection empowers you to respond to life's stressors with resilience and grace, knowing that your body is an ally in your healing journey.

Despite the healing potential of somatic practices, challenges can arise, particularly when beginning this work. Trust in the therapeutic process is crucial, yet it can be daunting to surrender to the sensations and emotions that surface. It's essential to approach somatic work with an open mind and patience, allowing yourself to explore comfortably. Ensuring a safe environment for exploration is equally vital. Whether working with a trained coach or practicing independently, create a space where you feel secure and supported. This might involve surrounding yourself with familiar objects, playing soothing music, or setting boundaries to protect your time and energy. It's important to remind yourself that whatever emotions or tremors come up, not stop them but accept them as they are released. By fostering trust and safety, you create a fertile ground for healing, where you can fully engage with the transformative power of somatic practices.

Mindfulness Practices for Emotional Balance

Mindfulness is like taking a gentle pause in the chaos of daily life, allowing you to reconnect with the present moment. It involves active, open attention to the present, observing your thoughts and feelings without judgment. Being fully present in the moment, coupled with nonjudgmental awareness, forms the cornerstone of mindfulness. By embracing this practice, you cultivate an emotional equilibrium that can transform your relationship with yourself and the world around you. Mindfulness encourages you to let go of past regrets and future anxieties, focusing instead on the here and now. This shift in perspective can be incredibly liberating, as it frees you from the weight of constant analysis and self-criticism.

Incorporating mindfulness into your life doesn't require grand gestures or secluded retreats. Simple, daily practices can make mindfulness accessible and manageable. Start with **breath awareness**, a foundational mindfulness exercise that centers on the rhythm of your breath. Take a few moments each day to focus solely on your breathing, noticing the sensations of each inhale and exhale. This practice anchors you to the present, offering a respite from racing thoughts.

Another effective technique is **body scan meditation**, where you mentally travel through each part of your body, noting any sensations or tensions. This meditation fosters a connection between mind and body, enhancing self-awareness and relaxation. These simple yet profound exercises offer a pathway to a more mindful existence.

Mindfulness significantly impacts emotional regulation, offering tools to manage emotional responses more quickly. Practicing mindfulness can reduce stress and anxiety, which are frequent companions of modern life. The nonjudgmental nature of mindfulness allows you to observe emotions without getting swept away by them. This detachment fosters emotional resilience, enabling you to respond to challenges calmly and clearly. As you cultivate mindfulness, you might notice a shift in how you experience emotions. They become less overwhelming—more like passing waves rather than storms. This change empowers you to navigate life's ups and downs with grace and stability.

Integrating mindfulness into daily routines can be both practical and rewarding. Consider adopting mindful eating practices, where you fully engage with the experience of eating. Pay attention to each bite's flavors, textures, and sensations, savoring the nourishment it provides. This practice turns a mundane task into an opportunity for mindfulness, promoting a deeper connection with your body. Similarly, mindfulness can be woven into daily chores, transforming them from mindless activities into mindful moments. Whether washing dishes or folding laundry, focus on the sensations and actions involved. These practices remind you that mindfulness isn't confined to meditation cushions; it's a way of being that permeates every aspect of life. Making mindfulness a part of your daily routine creates a more intentional, peaceful, and balanced lif e.

Art Therapy: Healing Through Creativity

Art therapy stands out as a nonverbal, creative pathway to healing that taps into the depths of the human soul. It offers a form of expression transcending words, providing a canvas for emotions to flow freely. Through art, you can reflect on your inner self, capturing the nuances of feelings that often elude verbal expression. This form of therapy invites you to explore your creative instincts, encouraging you to let your guard down and connect with the parts of yourself that may have been silenced. Art becomes a mirror, reflecting emotions that are sometimes too complex to articulate, allowing you to engage with them in a tangible, meaningful way.

Engaging in art therapy doesn't require you to be an artist. Simple exercises can facilitate profound self-exploration and healing. Start by drawing a portrait of your inner child. Let your instincts guide you as you sketch, focusing on the arising emotions. This exercise can uncover hidden aspects of your inner world, offering insights into your current emotional state. Collage-making is another powerful technique for self-expression. Gather images and words that resonate with you, authentically arranging them. As you create, notice the themes that emerge. These collages can be visual diaries, chronicling your emotional journey and providing a snapshot of your inner landscape.

The therapeutic benefits of creativity are multifaceted. Engaging in art can be a cathartic release, allowing you to process emotions stored within. Creating can bring relief, helping unearth and dissipate tension or anxiety. Art also enables you to gain new perspectives, offering a different lens through which to view your experiences. By stepping outside the confines of language, you can explore your emotions with a fresh perspective, uncovering layers of understanding that might otherwise remain hidden. This process fosters emotional insight, helping you to navigate your feelings with greater clarity and confidence.

Many individuals have experienced significant breakthroughs through art therapy. One woman found solace in painting after years of struggling with anxiety. Each brushstroke became a step toward healing, allowing her to express fears and hopes that words could not capture. Another discovered a newfound sense of freedom through collage, using it as a tool to explore and redefine her identity. These success stories illustrate the transformative power of creativity, highlighting its ability to unlock emotions and promote healing. Art therapy provides a sanctuary where you can explore your inner world openly and acceptably, inviting healing to unfold naturally.

As you embrace the healing power of creativity, remember that art is a personal and evolving process. It allows you to explore, express, and understand aspects of yourself that words may not reach. This chapter on art therapy serves as a reminder of the innate potential within you to transform and heal. Your creative journey is unique, and engaging in these practices opens the door to deeper self-awareness and emotional freedom. With each creation, you step toward healing, building a bridge between your inner child and the person you are today.

CHAPTER THREE

BUILDING SELF-LOVE VIA INNER CHILD HEALING

"The relationship you have with yourself is the foundation for all other relationships." Mel Robbins

Have you ever looked in the mirror and struggled to find something kind to say about yourself? That moment of silent judgment, where self-criticism runs rampant, is all too familiar for many of us. It's as if the internal critic has a megaphone, drowning out any whispers of kindness we might offer ourselves. This tendency to judge ourselves harshly is deeply ingrained, but it doesn't have to define us. Self-compassion provides an alternative, a way to reduce the volume of self-criticism and amplify the voice of kindness. Unlike self-esteem, which often depends on comparing ourselves to others, self-compassion is about embracing who we are, flaws and all. It's a practice of self-kindness, recognizing our shared humanity, and maintaining mindfulness.

As defined by researcher Kristin Neff, self-compassion involves treating ourselves with the same empathy and understanding we would extend to a friend. It encourages self-kindness over self-criticism, offering warmth and acceptance rather than harsh judgment. When you practice self-compassion, you acknowledge that *everyone* struggles and makes mistakes. This recognition of common humanity reminds you that you are not alone in your imperfections. Mindfulness, another core principle of self-compassion, involves observing your thoughts and emotions without getting swept away. It allows you to balance your experiences, avoiding the trap of over-identification, where you become consumed by negative feelings. Through self-compassion, you learn to sit with discomfort and uncertainty, offering yourself the grace you deserve.

Cultivating self-compassion requires intention and practice, but the rewards are significant. One exercise to develop this kinder relationship with yourself is loving-kindness meditation. This practice involves silently repeating phrases of goodwill, first toward yourself and then extending them to others.

Interactive Exercise: Practicing Self-Compassion Using Loving Kindness Meditation

Objective: Cultivate a compassionate mindset toward yourself and others.

Instructions:

1. **Settle in.** Find a quiet, comfortable space where you won't be disturbed.

2. Perform loving-kindness meditation. Close your eyes and take a few deep breaths. Your hands can rest on your lap, or you can have one hand in your heart area and the other one in your stomach. Repeat the following phrases silently to yourself:

"May I be happy."

"May I be healthy."

"May I be safe."

"May I be at peace."

3. Extend compassion. Gradually extend these wishes to others, including friends, family, and even those you find difficult.

4. Reflect. Spend a few moments noticing how this practice makes you feel.

Engage in this exercise regularly, allowing the warmth of compassion to permeate your thoughts and actions.

This meditation nurtures a sense of connection and empathy for yourself and others.

If you want an audio version of a similar Loving Kindness Meditation, follow the QR code below to download it to your phone:

Or go to the website: https://www.michelleduffy1111.com/aud iosforhealingyourinnerchildbook

Another practice is self-compassionate letter writing. Take a moment to write a letter to yourself from the perspective of a compassionate friend. Acknowledge your struggles, offer understanding, and express encouragement. This exercise can be a powerful reminder of your innate worth and resilience.

Interactive Exercise: Self-compassionate Letter Writing

Objective: Cultivate self-worth and resilience.

Instructions:

1. **Settle in.** Find a quiet, comfortable space where you won't be disturbed. Gather any pens, coloring pencils, and paper utensils you will use here.

2. **Identify the situation.** Focus on a specific issue troubling you. It can be a mistake, an argument, a time you had self-doubt, or anything that triggers feelings of shame, guilt, and inadequacy. Simply notice this mentally.

3. **Write as a compassionate friend would.** It often helps to imagine someone who loves you profoundly or someone you love unconditionally, like a child. If it's your best friend and she

is loving and understanding, she will give you words of encouragement, love, and compassion. Begin writing to yourself with this in mind.

4. **Approach with nonjudgment and validation.** Start by acknowledging and validating your emotions. Instead of judging yourself, simply state how you feel and why. For example, "I know you feel sad and disappointed because you think you should have done better. That's understandable, and it's okay to feel this way."

5. **Reframe the situation.** Besides encouraging yourself, see if you can reframe the negative to a positive. This can be something like: "Even though things didn't go as planned, this experience helped me grow. I trust that things will be better." Reframing helps to form new neuron connections to these new thoughts that evoke positive feelings like a sense of peace and resilience.

6. **End on a positive note.** Close your letter with love and acceptance. You might remind yourself that you are stronger than you think or say, "Give it time. Take it one day at a time. You've got this! I love you."

The benefits of self-compassion extend far beyond emotional comfort. Research by Kristin Neff indicates that self-compassion can reduce anxiety and depression, providing a buffer against the stresses of daily life. Treating yourself with kindness improves your emotional regulation, allowing you to respond to challenges more efficiently. Self-compassion fosters resilience, helping you recover from setbacks with hope and determination. It encourages a growth mindset, where failures become opportunities for learning rather than sources of shame. By embracing self-compassion, you cultivate inner strength, empowering yourself to face life's uncertainties confidently and gracefully.

Despite its benefits, self-compassion often needs to be understood. Some view it as self-indulgent, fearing that being kind to themselves will lead to complacency or laziness. However, self-compassion is not about letting yourself off the hook; it's about holding yourself accountable *with* kindness. It encourages you to strive toward your goals while acknowledging your limitations. Others confuse self-compassion with selfishness, believing it prioritizes personal needs over those of others. In reality, self-compassion enhances your capacity for empathy and connection. By nurturing yourself, you become more available and present for those around you. Understanding these distinctions is crucial, as it allows you to embrace self-compassion without reservation, knowing that it enriches your life and those you touch.

Overcoming Negative Self-Talk

You might not remember exactly when it started, but that critical voice in your head became a familiar companion somewhere along the way. It whispers doubts and magnifies mistakes, often echoing the criticisms you heard as a child. These internalized messages stem from caregivers who, perhaps unintentionally, instilled a sense of inadequacy. It could have been a teacher's comment or a peer's taunt that took root and grew into a belief. Society, too, plays a role with its relentless standards of success and beauty that make self-acceptance feel like an uphill battle. This confluence of influences shapes the narrative you tell yourself, often turning it into a loop of self-doubt and criticism. Understanding these origins is the first step in dismantling their power, and it's crucial to recognize that these thoughts, though persistent, are not immutable truths.

To counteract this negative self-talk, cognitive restructuring provides a framework for change. This technique involves identifying distorted beliefs and replacing them with more balanced thoughts. Start by noticing when a negative thought arises, such as "I'll never be good enough." Challenge this by asking if it's genuinely accurate or just a habit of thinking. Consider the evidence contradicting this belief—moments of success or praise you've received. Positive self-affirmations can further reinforce this shift. Craft affirmations that resonate with you, like "I am worthy of love and respect." Repeat them regularly, allowing these affirmations to weave into your subconscious.

Interactive Exercise: Crafting Your Affirmations

Objective: Know how to craft affirmations to overcome negative self-talk and more.

Instructions: Affirmations are statements in the first person, such as, "I am beautiful." Auto-suggestions are statements in the third person, such as, "You are beautiful."

Both affirmations and auto-suggestions work to influence your subconscious; however, affirmations are more powerful. They evoke a more vital emotion and use one of the most potent subconscious levels, the identity level, with the words "I AM."

What to keep in mind when writing affirmations:

1. The affirmation must be written in the present moment. This is because the subconscious mind, where we are impressing this belief, only understands the present tense.

2. The affirmation must be positive in tone and words. Instead of "I am not lazy," you would say, "I am persistent and finish my work." The latter is more positive and does not have the negative word "not." The subconscious does not understand negatives, so never put in your affirmations words like "not" or "no."

3. The affirmation must evoke emotion. Use your words and play around with the phrases you need for self-love, authenticity, or anything else you need or want.

4. Finally, affirmations work by repetition. They seep into your subconscious with repetition. Say them first thing in the morning or right before bed, as this is when your mind is most suggestible. You can also have them written down where you can see them, like in your bathroom mirror when brushing your teeth or on your computer screen when you begin to work.

Transforming negative self-talk into positive affirmations enhances your self-esteem and emotional well-being. As you cultivate a more supportive inner dialogue, you may notice a gradual increase in self-confidence. The internal critic loses its grip, making room for a kinder, more encouraging voice. This shift strengthens your self-worth, reinforcing the belief that you deserve love and success. With time, positive self-talk becomes a foundation for resilience, enabling you to navigate challenges more easily. It fosters a sense of inner peace and contentment, allowing you to embrace your strengths and imperfections. As you nurture this compassionate relationship with yourself, you unlock the potential for profound personal growth and fulfillment.

Journaling for Self-Discovery and Growth

Consider opening a blank page and letting your thoughts spill out, un-filtered and unjudged. This is the essence of journaling, a practice that is a substantial tool for self-discovery. Reflective writing invites you to look inward, exploring the depths of your thoughts and emotions. It's a space where introspection reigns, allowing you to uncover layers of your subconscious that might otherwise remain hidden. Through this process, your words become a mirror, reflecting patterns and beliefs that guide your actions. It offers clarity, helping you see the threads of your life woven into a tapestry of experiences and insights. Whether you're capturing fleeting thoughts or delving into deeper reflections, journaling is a dialogue with yourself, one that fosters growth and understanding.

To harness the power of journaling, incorporate specific tech-niques designed to encourage self-exploration. **Stream-of-conscious-ness writing** is a liberating practice where you write continuously with-out worrying about grammar or coherence. This free-flowing method taps into your subconscious, revealing thoughts and feelings you might not have been aware of. I recommend writing with pen and paper rather than typing on the computer. There's scientific evidence that handwriting is better for connecting to our emotions because it's natural and creative and an activity we have done since we were young. The touching of the paper and the free flow of doodling or images with your writing make the experience more immersive. It also engages both brain hemispheres instead of typing in the computer, which exclusively uses the left brain hemisphere. Using the left hemisphere (logic and language) and the right hemisphere (creativity and emotions) simultaneously makes inner child healing more effective.

Gratitude journaling is another powerful tool. You cultivate appreciation and positivity by noting things you're thankful for daily. This practice shifts your focus from what's lacking to what's abundant, fostering a sense of contentment. Future self-visualization exercises invite you to see your life as you wish, encouraging you to set intentions and visualize the steps needed to achieve them. These techniques transform writing from a simple activity into a catalyst for personal growth, guiding you toward a deeper understanding of yourself.

Regular journaling offers a wealth of benefits, enhancing self-awareness and personal development. You gain a clearer picture of your inner world as you consistently engage with your thoughts and emotions. This heightened awareness allows you to recognize patterns, beliefs, and tendencies that shape your behavior. Emotional clarity emerges as you unravel the complexities of your feelings, paving the way for healthier emotional regulation. Journaling becomes a safe space to process experiences, work through challenges, and celebrate triumphs. Over time, this practice fosters a sense of empowerment as you take ownership of your narrative and shape it with intention. The act of regularly putting pen to paper becomes a ritual of self-care, one that nurtures growth and transformation.

Many individuals have discovered the profound influence of journaling, using it as a tool for self-discovery and healing. One woman I know used it to navigate a challenging life transition. She could process her fears and anxieties through daily entries, ultimately finding clarity and direction. Her journal became a trusted confidante, offering solace and perspective during difficult times. Another client found that this free-flow writing helped her uncover subconscious beliefs about self-worth that had been holding her back. By exploring these beliefs on paper, she was able to challenge and reframe them, leading to a newfound sense of confidence. These success stories illustrate the potential of journaling to bring about meaningful personal insights and growth. They remind us that within the journal pages lies the potential for transformation, waiting to be discovered.

Journaling is a practice that invites you to pause, reflect, and connect with yourself on a deeper level. It's a journey of exploration that encourages you to embrace your thoughts and emotions with curiosity and compassion. As you engage with this practice, you create a space where self-discovery and growth can flourish, leading to a more authentic and fulfilling life.

Embracing Imperfection: The Path to Authenticity

Embracing imperfection can feel radical in a world that often equates worth with flawless achievement. Yet, it is within this acceptance of our flaws that true self-love flourishes. Letting go of perfectionism means releasing the constant pressure to meet an unattainable standard. It involves recognizing that mistakes and missteps are part of the human experience, not marks against our character. By valuing authenticity over approval, we free ourselves from the exhausting pursuit of external validation. Authenticity allows you to show up as you are without the need to mask your vulnerabilities. In this space, you can nurture a self-love that is genuine and unwavering, rooted in the acceptance of your entire self.

To foster acceptance of your imperfections, engaging in practical exercises can be transformative. Consider starting with imperfection writing prompts, where you reflect on moments of perceived failure and rewrite them as opportunities for growth. This practice encourages a shift in perspective, viewing imperfections not as flaws but as stepping stones in your journey. Practicing vulnerability in safe settings also plays a crucial role. Share your struggles and uncertainties with trusted friends or support groups. In doing so, you'll discover the strength in vulnerability and the relief from being seen and accepted for who you are. These exercises foster a sense of belonging and connection, reminding you that imperfection is not something to hide but to embrace.

Interactive Exercise: Journaling Prompts for Releasing Imperfection

- Write about a time when you felt the need to be perfect. What was driving this feeling, and how did it impact you?

- List three imperfections or traits you've often felt self-conscious about. How might these qualities be strengths or add to your uniqueness?

- Describe a flaw or mistake you've made recently. What did it teach you about yourself, and how could you see it with compassion?

- What negative self-beliefs do you hold about your imperfections? Where do you think these beliefs came from?

- Think of someone you love who has imperfections. How do you view their flaws, and how might you apply this kindness to yourself?

- Imagine your life without the pressure to be perfect. What would change? What risks would you take, and how would you spend your time?

Embracing imperfections paves the way for a more genuine and fulfilling life. Cultivating self-acceptance allows you to shed the masks you've worn to fit societal expectations, revealing your true self beneath. This authenticity attracts meaningful connections, encouraging others to do the same. When you embrace your imperfections, you invite others to foster deeper relationships built on honesty and understanding. The walls of pretense crumble, replaced by the warmth of genuine connection. By accepting yourself as you are, you create a life that resonates with your actual values and desires, leading to greater fulfillment and joy.

Reflect on the stories of individuals who have found strength in their imperfections. Think of Brené Brown, who has built a career by embracing vulnerability and imperfection as power sources. Her work has shown us that being open about our struggles fosters resilience and connection. Similarly, think of J.K. Rowling, whose early rejections became the foundation for her later successes. Her story of perseverance in the face of adversity inspires countless others to embrace their imperfections as catalysts for growth. On a more personal level, I recall a friend who openly shared her battle with anxiety, transforming her vulnerability into a source of strength. Her willingness to embrace her imperfections inspired those around her, creating a ripple effect of authenticity and acceptance.

In a society that often demands perfection, embracing imperfection is an act of defiance. It is a declaration that self-love is not contingent on flawless achievement but on accepting our humanity. Letting go of perfectionism and valuing authenticity over approval opens the door to a life rich with meaning and connection. Through practical exercises like journaling and practicing vulnerability, you cultivate richer self-acceptance, allowing your true self to shine. As you embrace your imperfections, you create space for authenticity to flourish, leading to stronger relationships and a more fulfilling life. In doing so, you join a chorus of voices who have discovered the power of imperfection, finding strength and beauty in their most authentic selves.

Daily Self-Love Rituals

Envision starting your day with a gentle reminder of your worth, a moment dedicated solely to acknowledging your strengths and intentions. This is the essence of daily self-love rituals and practices that anchor you in a rhythm of care and compassion. *Regular* rituals are the foundation of self-love, weaving a tapestry of well-being that supports you through life's ups and downs. Consistency is key here. Just as you wouldn't skip brushing your teeth, self-care becomes a nonnegotiable part of your routine, a commitment to nurturing your soul. Building a self-love routine is about creating a daily practice that resonates with you, one that feeds your spirit and aligns with your values. These rituals become a touchstone, a way to reset and ground yourself amid the noise and chaos.

Incorporating simple self-love rituals into your daily life doesn't require grand gestures or elaborate plans. It's about finding small, meaningful moments that speak to your heart. Contemplate starting your morning with a gratitude list, jotting down a few things you're thankful for as you sip your coffee. This practice sets a positive tone for the day, shifting your focus to abundance rather than lack. In the evening, reflect and relax, taking a few minutes to unwind and acknowledge the day's experiences. Whether it's a warm bath, a few pages of a favorite book, or simply sitting in silence, these unwinding moments create a buffer between the day's demands and the peace of the night. Self-care check-ins throughout the day can also be invaluable. One of my favorites is a 15-minute grounding (walking barefoot in the grass) after having lunch. Pause to ask yourself, "What do I need right now?" This simple question invites you to listen to your body and mind, guiding you toward actions that support your well-being.

The benefits of these routine self-love practices are substantial, permeating every aspect of your life. As you consistently engage in these rituals, you'll likely notice a reduction in stress levels, as if the world's weight has lifted just a bit. These moments of care cultivate an increased sense of peace, a calm that carries you through challenges with grace and resilience. The regularity of self-love rituals fosters emotional stability, providing a steady anchor when life's seas become turbulent. They remind you that you are worthy of care and attention, reinforcing a positive relationship *with yourself*. As these practices become second nature, you'll find that happiness and contentment are not fleeting states but enduring companions.

Maintaining self-love rituals amid a busy lifestyle requires intention and flexibility. Start by setting aside dedicated time for these practices, even just **five minutes daily.** Treat this time as sacred, a *nonnegotiable* appointment with yourself. Adapt your rituals to fit your personal needs and schedule. If mornings are hectic, shift your gratitude practice to lunch breaks or evenings. The key is to create authentic and sustainable rituals you look forward to rather than view as another task on your to-do list. Remember, self-love is not about perfection but about presence. It's about showing up for yourself in whatever way feels right and acknowledging that your needs may shift and evolve. By making these rituals a priority, you cultivate a life that is rich with self-love and well-being.

Celebrating Small Wins: Building Confidence

In the hustle and bustle of daily life, it's easy to overlook the small victories that punctuate our journey. Yet, recognizing these achievements is crucial for building confidence. Each small win reinforces positive behavior, encouraging you to progress toward your goals. Picture the satisfaction of completing a challenging task at work or sticking to a new habit for a week. These moments, though seemingly minor, are the building blocks of self-assurance. Acknowledging them affirms your capabilities, strengthening your belief in yourself. Celebrating small wins shifts the focus from what you haven't achieved to what you have, creating a positive cycle of motivation and achievement. It's about recognizing the effort and dedication you put into reaching each milestone, however small it may seem. This practice fosters an environment where growth and learning are celebrated, paving the way for continued success.

There are many ways you can acknowledge and celebrate these personal achievements. One effective method is keeping a **success journal**. In this journal, note down every accomplishment, no matter how small. Write it down, whether it's finishing a book, completing a workout, or having a difficult conversation. Over time, this record becomes a powerful testament to your growth, a reminder of your progress. Another strategy is rewarding yourself with meaningful treats. These rewards don't need to be extravagant—perhaps a favorite snack, a relaxing bath, or an episode of your beloved TV show. The key is to connect the reward to the achievement, reinforcing the behavior you want to continue. Sharing your achievements with a support network can also be incredibly rewarding. Tell a friend, partner, or family member about your success. Their encouragement and pride can amplify your sense of accomplishment, creating a supportive space for your journey.

The impact of celebrating small wins is cumulative, gradually leading to significant personal growth. Each small success builds momentum, propelling you forward with renewed energy and purpose. This momentum fuels your motivation, making it easier to tackle more significant challenges. As you celebrate these wins, you strengthen your self-efficacy, the belief in your ability to achieve your goals. This growing confidence becomes a powerful force, helping you overcome obstacles and setbacks with resilience. Over time, accumulating small victories contributes to a radical transformation as you realize you are capable of more than you ever imagined. By focusing on what you can achieve rather than what you can't, you create a mindset of possibility and potential.

The science of this stems from "confirmation bias" in psychology. When you focus on a thought or belief, confirmation bias leads you to seek evidence that reinforces this focus, creating a self-perpetuating cycle. For example, consider someone who believes they are "not good enough" in social situations. Because of this belief, this person might enter social interactions expecting to feel awkward or to say something wrong. During a conversation, if they accidentally stumble over a word or notice someone checking their phone, they interpret these events as signs that they're indeed "not good enough" in social settings.

The person then focuses on these minor moments as proof of their belief, ignoring or discounting any positive interactions they have, such as people smiling, engaging in conversation, or responding warmly. They might even overlook times when they feel confident or make someone laugh. Over time, this *selective focus* reinforces their belief, creating a cycle where they continually "find" evidence of their perceived inadequacy, reinforcing their negative self-view.

I like to remind my clients that **"what you focus on expands"**—which is the same thing as "confirmation bias." That's why celebrating wins is vital for any inner healing journey. Focus on what you're doing right, and you'll get more of it.

Reflect on the experiences of those who have achieved personal growth by acknowledging their small victories. There's the woman who decided to start running after years of self-doubt. She began with short jogs around her neighborhood, celebrating each time she went a little further. Over time, these small victories led to her completing a half-marathon, a feat she once thought impossible. Her confidence grew with each step, transforming her perception of herself and what she could achieve.

Embracing and celebrating small wins is a powerful strategy for building confidence and fostering personal growth. Recognizing and rewarding your achievements creates a positive feedback loop that encourages ongoing progress. No matter how small, each victory contributes to a cumulative effect, strengthening your self-efficacy and momentum. Acknowledging your successes, you pave the way for *significant* personal transformation, discovering new strengths and capabilities. This practice enhances your confidence and fosters a sense of fulfillment and joy in the journey.

By recognizing small wins, you create a life that celebrates growth and possibility, empowering you to reach new heights. As you turn the page to explore overcoming trust issues, remember that each step forward is a victory worth celebrating, building the foundation for a life rich with confidence and success.

Chapter Four

OVERCOMING TRUST ISSUES THROUGH INNER CHILD WORK

"When we heal the child within, we unlock the ability to trust again."
John Bradshaw

As a child, I remember holding tightly to a small, tattered teddy bear, believing it would protect me from the shadows in my room at night. That bear was my first experience of trust—something tangible and comforting in a world that often felt uncertain. As I grew, the simplicity of that trust faded, replaced by more complex emotions and experiences that challenged my ability to trust others and myself. Trust, I learned, is not always easy. It's a fragile thing, quickly shattered by betrayals or disappointments, yet it is the foundation upon which we build our relationships and sense of self. For many women, the journey to trusting others begins with learning to trust ourselves. This chapter explores how self-trust can become a reliable cornerstone in your life.

Self-trust is the bedrock upon which *all* other forms of trust are built. When you trust yourself, you cultivate confidence in your decision-making, allowing you to navigate life's complexities confidently. This self-reliance fosters independence, empowering you to stand tall even in the face of adversity. Without self-trust, doubt can creep in, eroding your sense of stability and making it difficult to trust others. Building self-trust requires listening to your inner voice and honoring your truth, even when it feels inconvenient or challenging. It involves recognizing that your experiences and emotions deserve space and consideration.

You can engage in practical activities reinforcing your belief in yourself to enhance self-trust. Begin with daily affirmations for self-assurance, repeating positive statements that affirm your worth and capabilities. These affirmations remind you of your inner strength, building a foundation of confidence that underpins your actions. Reflective journaling on past successes is another vital tool. Record moments when you overcame challenges or made decisions that led to positive outcomes. This practice helps you gather evidence of your resilience and wisdom, reinforcing your ability to trust your judgment. Regularly engaging in these exercises creates a narrative of competence and reliability, strengthening your self-trust.

The impact of self-trust on personal growth is profound. As you cultivate trust in yourself, your self-esteem flourishes, allowing you to approach life's challenges with a sense of empowerment. This self-assuredness bolsters your resilience, enabling you to bounce back from setbacks quickly. You become more willing to take risks, knowing you have the inner resources to handle whatever comes your way. This growth in self-trust transforms your relationship with yourself, fostering a sense of wholeness and integrity that permeates every aspect of your life. As you develop self-trust, you lay the groundwork for deeper connections with others, as your confidence inspires trust and respect in those around you.

There is a notable relationship between self-trust and intuition. Trusting yourself enhances your ability to listen to your inner guidance, the quiet voice that often knows what is best for you. This intuitive decision-making allows you to act with clarity and conviction, even when circumstances are uncertain. By trusting your gut feelings, you align your actions with your authentic self, creating a life reflecting your values and desires. This alignment fosters a sense of peace and fulfillment as you navigate your path with confidence and purpose. As you deepen your self-trust, you strengthen your connection to your intuition, empowering you to make decisions that honor your highest good.

Interactive Exercise: Building Self-Trust

Objective: Reinforce your self-trust through daily practices.
   Instructions:

   1. **Morning Affirmations:** Each morning, stand in front of a mirror and speak three affirmations aloud, such as "I trust myself to make wise decisions," "I am capable and strong," and "I honor my inner voice."

   2. **Evening Reflection:** Before bed, write about your day's decision and reflect on its outcome. Note what it taught you about your capabilities and judgment.

   3. **Weekly Review:** Review your journal entries and affirmations

at the end of each week. Identify patterns of success and areas where self-trust helped you overcome challenges.

By consistently practicing these exercises, you nurture a strong foundation of self-trust, empowering you to face life's uncertainties with courage and confidence.

Reframing Past Betrayals

When betrayal first hits, it feels like the world has shifted beneath your feet. The ground that once seemed solid becomes a landscape of uncertainty and doubt. You might find yourself questioning everything you believed about trust and safety. This experience leaves emotional scars, deep and raw, that often lead to a pervasive fear of vulnerability. Betrayal can be a subtle whisper or a roar, but its impact remains substantial. Trust becomes a fragile thread, easily frayed by the winds of past hurts. These emotional wounds can create barriers that make trusting others seem impossible. The fear of opening up, only to be hurt again, can paralyze you, keeping you locked within the walls of self-protection.

Yet, within the pain of betrayal lies the potential for growth and healing. Reframing these experiences is a powerful way to transform them from sources of anguish into opportunities for strength. One effective strategy is cognitive reframing exercises, which involve looking at the betrayal from different perspectives. This doesn't mean excusing the betrayal but understanding its place in the broader story of your life. Ask yourself what the experience taught you about your values, boundaries, and needs. *Identifying lessons learned from betrayal allows you to extract meaning from the pain.* You might discover a newfound understanding of what you truly value in relationships or a clearer sense of the boundaries you need to protect yourself. These insights can serve as guiding lights, illuminating the path toward healthier connections.

Releasing resentment is a crucial step in rebuilding trust. Holding on to anger and bitterness might feel like a protective shield, but in reality, it chains you to the past. This emotional weight hinders your ability to move forward, clouding your interactions with doubt and suspicion. Practices for emotional release, such as expressive writing or mindfulness meditation, can help you let go of these burdens. Writing about your feelings allows you to process and release pent-up emotions, creating space for healing. Mindfulness meditation, on the other hand, encourages you to observe your feelings without judgment, fostering acceptance and peace. Forgiveness plays a pivotal role in this process. Forgiveness is a tool for liberation, enabling you to reclaim your power and choose how you want to move forward.

Contemplate the stories of individuals who have successfully reframed betrayal and rebuilt trust. One woman I knew faced a devastating betrayal in her marriage, which left her questioning her worth and ability to trust. Through introspection and journaling, she began to reframe the betrayal as a catalyst for personal growth. She realized that the experience had taught her the importance of self-respect and boundaries. With time and reflection, she forgave her partner—not to reconcile, but to release herself from the bitterness that held her back. Another friend faced betrayal in a professional setting, where a trusted colleague undermined her work. Initially, she felt crushed and humiliated but turned to cognitive reframing to find a different perspective. She identified the lessons learned, such as clear communication and self-advocacy. She rebuilt her professional relationships by releasing resentment and strengthening her confidence and resilience.

These stories remind us that painful betrayal does not define us. It is through the process of reframing and releasing that we find healing and strength. The journey is not easy, but each step forward is a testament to your resilience and capacity for growth. By transforming the narrative of betrayal, you open the door to new possibilities where trust can flourish again.

Safe Vulnerability: Opening Up Without Fear

Vulnerability is often misunderstood as a weakness, but it is one of the greatest strengths you can possess. It means showing others your true self, complete with flaws and fears. This authenticity is the bedrock of trust. When you allow yourself to be vulnerable, you open the door to authentic self-expression. You invite others to connect with you deeper, beyond the superficial exchanges that often dominate our interactions. This openness creates a space where genuine connections can flourish. Choosing vulnerability is a courageous act in a world that usually encourages us to wear masks and hide our true feelings. It signals to those around you that you trust them enough to be your authentic self, inviting them to do the same. This mutual exchange fosters a sense of belonging and acceptance, strengthening bonds and building trust.

Expressing vulnerability, however, should be approached with care to ensure it is safe and supportive. Setting emotional boundaries is a crucial first step. These boundaries are guidelines for how much you share and with whom, ensuring your vulnerability is met with respect and understanding. Gradual disclosure is another strategy to help you express vulnerability without fear of judgment. Open up slowly, sharing small pieces of yourself initially, and gauging the response. As trust builds, you can reveal more confidence in the safety of the connection. This measured approach allows you to protect yourself while still engaging in meaningful exchanges. Setting these parameters creates an environment where vulnerability is met with empathy and acceptance rather than criticism or dismissal.

The benefits of embracing vulnerability in relationships are transformative. You foster emotional intimacy and connection when you are open and honest. These threads weave *strong* relational bonds, providing security and warmth. Vulnerability invites others to see you as you are, encouraging them to do the same. This reciprocal openness deepens trust, as both parties feel valued and understood. In this space, relationships thrive, free from the constraints of pretension or fear. The bonds formed through vulnerability are resilient and capable of weathering the storms of life with grace and strength. By nurturing this openness, you create a sanctuary where you and your loved ones can grow and support one another through life's challenges.

Despite its benefits, the fear of vulnerability often holds many back. The concern about appearing weak or being rejected is a common barrier. It whispers that showing your true self might lead to judgment or exclusion. This fear can paralyze you from reaching out or forming meaningful connections. It's essential to recognize that these fears, while valid, do not define your worth or potential for connection. Vulnerability is not about exposing yourself indiscriminately; it's about choosing to be open in safe and supportive spaces. By acknowledging these fears, you empower yourself to move beyond them, embracing the strength and courage that vulnerability brings. Remember that vulnerability is a choice you make on your terms, in your own time.

Once, I met a woman who had been deeply hurt in a past relationship. Her fear of vulnerability was palpable, as she worried that opening up might lead to more heartache. Through gradual disclosure and setting clear boundaries, she began to share her feelings with a trusted friend. Over time, she realized that her vulnerability was met with understanding and support, not judgment. This experience transformed her perspective, showing her that being open did not equate to weakness. Instead, it empowered her to form more meaningful connections. Her story is a testament to the power of vulnerability, demonstrating that it is not a sign of weakness but a pathway to strength and trust.

Embracing vulnerability is an act of courage. It's about showing up as your true self, even when it feels uncomfortable or risky. Doing so invites others to connect with you deeper, creating a foundation of trust and understanding.

Trust-Building Practices in Relationships

Building trust in relationships is like tending to a garden. It requires consistent attention and care to flourish. At the heart of this process is communication, the lifeline that keeps relationships thriving. Regular, open conversations lay the groundwork for trust, allowing partners to express their needs, desires, and concerns without fear. This level of transparency fosters an environment where honesty can thrive, creating a strong and resilient foundation. When you and your partner communicate honestly, you establish a shared understanding that becomes the bedrock of your relationship. This transparency ensures that both parties feel heard and valued, reducing the likelihood of misunderstandings or resentment. Consistent communication is not just about speaking; it's about listening with an open heart and mind, which allows trust to deepen and relationships to grow.

Reliability and dependability are the unsung heroes of trust-building. These qualities underscore your promises, demonstrating that your words are not empty but backed by action. When you follow through on commitments, big or small, you signal to your partner that they can rely on you. This consistency builds a sense of security, knowing you will be there when needed. Being present and attentive, too, plays a crucial role. It means showing up physically and emotionally and engaging fully in shared moments. This presence reassures your partner they are a priority, reinforcing the trust in your relationship. By embodying reliability and dependability, you create a safe space where trust can flourish, free from the shadows of doubt and uncertainty.

Trust-building is not just a passive process but an active pursuit that can be strengthened through practical exercises designed to enhance the bonds you share. Trust-building games and exercises can inject fun and engagement into this process. Consider activities like the "trust fall," where one partner leans back, trusting the other to catch them. While seemingly simple, these exercises can have lasting effects, reinforcing the trust that underpins your relationship. Joint goal-setting sessions offer another avenue for building trust. By sitting down together to outline shared goals, you create a collaborative vision for your future. This exercise encourages open dialogue about your hopes and dreams, aligning your paths and strengthening your partnership. These activities are about the actions and the connection they foster, reminding you of the trust you have built and continue to nurture.

Trust-building practices extend beyond romantic relationships, weaving into friendships and family dynamics. In friendships, trust is often built through shared experiences and mutual support. Regular check-ins and honest conversations allow friends to maintain connection, even when life's demands pull them in different directions. In family dynamics, trust is cultivated through dependability and presence. Being there for family members during difficult times and following through on promises demonstrates that trust is not just spoken but lived. These relationships are strengthened by consistently applying trust-building practices and creating networks of support that uplift and sustain.

Take into account the story of a couple at a crossroads, struggling to trust each other after a series of misunderstandings. They engaged in weekly check-ins, openly sharing their thoughts and feelings without judgment. This practice allowed them to rebuild their connection, gradually restoring the trust that had been frayed. Another example is a friendship tested by distance. Despite living miles apart, the two friends maintained their bond through regular phone calls and shared experiences, reinforcing the trust that had been the cornerstone of their relationship for years. These stories illustrate that trust is not a static quality but a dynamic process that requires ongoing attention and care. Trust can be nurtured and strengthened through consistent communication, honesty, and reliability, creating resilient and enduring relationships.

Releasing Control: Embracing Uncertainty

In our quest for stability, many of us cling tightly to control, believing it will shield us from the unpredictability of life. This instinct is understandable, especially when past experiences have left us vulnerable and exposed. Yet, this need for control can inadvertently undermine trust in ourselves and our relationships. When we insist on controlling every detail, we signal to those around us that we lack confidence in their abilities or intentions. This can create an environment where trust struggles to take root, as the implicit message is that others are unreliable partners in our shared journey. The fear of unpredictability often lies at the heart of this need for control. We resist change, preferring the safety of the known, even if it confines us. This resistance can become a prison of our own making, limiting our growth and the richness of our connections.

But there is freedom in letting go. Releasing control is not about surrendering responsibility but embracing life's flow with an open heart. One practical approach to letting go is through mindfulness practices. Mindfulness invites us to be present, to observe our thoughts and feelings without judgment, and to cultivate a sense of acceptance. As we practice mindfulness, we learn to detach from the need to dictate outcomes, allowing life to unfold naturally. This shift in perspective can reduce anxiety as we realize that we don't have to have all the answers. Embracing spontaneity and flexibility is another powerful strategy. When we allow ourselves to be open to change, we invite new experiences and possibilities. This openness can lead to unexpected joys and insights, enriching our lives in ways we never imagined. By practicing flexibility, we build the capacity to adapt, strengthening our resilience and trust.

The benefits of releasing control and embracing uncertainty are powerful. As we loosen our grip, we discover a world of possibilities hidden behind the walls of our own making. Our adaptability increases, allowing us to respond to life's challenges creatively and resourcefully. This enhanced creativity extends beyond problem-solving, infusing our lives with playfulness and wonder. We become more attuned to opportunities, seeing them as chances for growth rather than threats to our stability. This openness fosters a more profound connection in relationships, as we trust our partners to contribute their strengths and perspectives. By embracing change, we create space for trust to flourish, building dynamic and resilient relationships.

Of course, relinquishing control is not without its challenges. The anxiety of stepping into the unknown can be daunting, and it's natural to feel a sense of unease. Building confidence in uncertain situations requires patience and practice. Start by acknowledging your fears, recognizing that they are a normal part of the human experience. Then, focus on small steps that gradually expand your comfort zone. For example, try setting aside time each week to engage in an activity that pushes your boundaries, such as trying a new hobby or exploring a different part of town. These experiences build confidence, showing you can thrive even in unfamiliar settings. Surrounding yourself with supportive people can also make a significant difference. Sharing your concerns with trusted friends or a supportive community can provide reassurance and encouragement, reminding you that you are not alone in this journey.

Throughout this chapter, we've explored the complexities of trust, from the importance of self-trust to the courage required for vulnerability. As we release control and embrace uncertainty, we open ourselves to the richness of life, fostering trust and connection. Doing so lays the groundwork for deeper, more fulfilling relationships. As we transition to the next chapter, consider how these themes manifest in your life, guiding you toward healing and growth.

UNLOCK THE POWER OF GENEROSITY

"The best way to find yourself is to lose yourself in the service of others." - Mahatma Gandhi.

People who give without expecting anything in return live happier lives. So, let's make a difference together!

My mission is to make healing your inner child easy and empowering for every woman. But to reach more people, I need your help.

Most people choose books based on reviews. So, I'm asking you to help a fellow seeker on their journey of self-discovery by leaving a review.

It costs nothing and takes less than a minute, but it could change someone's healing journey. Your review could help...

...one more woman overcome her inner struggles and build self-love.

...one more soul break free from past wounds and create a peaceful life.

...one more person finds the courage to trust herself again.

...one more person reclaims the joy and freedom they deserve.

...one more dream come true.

To make a difference, simply scan the QR code below and leave a review:

https://www.amazon.com/review/review-your-purchases/?asin=B0DRZZBCCW

If you love helping others, you're my kind of person. Thank you from the bottom of my heart!

With unconditional love,

Michelle Duffy

Chapter Five

BREAKING NEGATIVE CYCLES THROUGH YOUR INNER CHILD

"The key to breaking patterns lies in understanding where they began."
Dr. Gabor Maté

Picture this: You're in a room full of mirrors, each reflecting a different version of yourself. Each mirror holds a story—some joyful, others filled with shadows. These reflections are like the patterns we carry from our past, especially destructive ones. They originate from childhood experiences that have shaped our perceptions and behaviors. Destructive patterns are those repetitive cycles that hold us back, often without realizing it. They manifest in various ways, such as recurring unhealthy relationships where you find yourself drawn to the same type of person who doesn't treat you well or self-defeating behaviors like procrastination or negative self-talk. These patterns become ingrained over time, fueled by the narratives we learned as children, telling us what to expect from the world and ourselves.

Recognizing these patterns is the first step in breaking them. This requires looking into those mirrors and seeing what is genuinely reflected. **Reflective journaling** can be a powerful tool in this process. By writing about your experiences, you can uncover the recurring themes and triggers perpetuating these cycles. Take into account prompts such as "What patterns do I notice in my relationships?" or "When do I feel most self-critical?" These questions can guide you in identifying the roots of your behaviors. Pattern recognition writing offers another approach, allowing you to map out your behaviors and see their connections. These exercises create a framework for understanding how past experiences influence present actions, providing a clearer picture of the patterns you wish to change.

These unaddressed patterns can be significant, affecting various areas of your life. In the professional realm, they may lead to setbacks, as self-doubt and fear of failure hinder your ability to seize opportunities or assert yourself. You might find yourself stuck in a job that doesn't fulfill you, unable to break free due to ingrained beliefs about your capabilities. Emotionally, these patterns can result in distress, manifesting as anxiety or depression. The weight of these unhealed patterns can leave you feeling trapped, as if you're living the same day on repeat. They can cloud your judgment and drain your energy, leaving little room for joy or growth. Recognizing the impact of these patterns is crucial for understanding the urgency of change.

Awareness is your greatest ally in disrupting these negative cycles. It involves mindfully observing behaviors and paying attention to your actions and reactions without judgment. This self-awareness allows you to catch yourself in repeating old patterns, creating a pause where you can choose a different path. Acknowledgment of emotional triggers is also essential. By identifying what prompts these patterns, you gain insight into their origins and can begin to address them at their root. This might involve understanding the fear behind your actions or recognizing the unmet needs that drive them. Self-awareness is not about self-criticism but about empowerment, offering you the clarity to make conscious choices that align with your true desires.

Interactive Exercise: Pattern Recognition Writing Prompts

Objective: Identify and understand personal destructive patterns.

Instructions:

1. **Reflect on patterns.** Write about the types of patterns you are experiencing. It can be people you're drawn to, behaviors (like procrastination, people-pleasing, emotional overeating, etc.), recurring thoughts (like negative self-talk), or emotional patterns (i.e., chronic anxiety, jealousy, frustration with others, etc.).

2. **Identify triggers.** Note any situations or environments that lead to these patterns.

3. **Explore the origins.** Can you remember the first time you felt, thought, or experienced that? It's normal if you can't think of the origin. This doesn't mean you won't break the pattern, but it is easier to do so when you remember the event's root.

4. **Consequences.** How has this pattern affected your life (with family, friends, professionally, etc.)?

5. **Reframe.** Now that you are aware of this trigger and the pattern it brings about, how are you choosing to respond the next time you get triggered in that way? (Note: This does not mean you will excel in doing this new thing the first time, but by thinking and writing down how you would like to respond instead of reacting, you are training your mind to feel this way, and with practice, you will get there).

6. **Implement new strategies.** If you struggle with negative self-talk, for instance, you can brainstorm ways to counteract this. For example, I will affirm and reframe when a negative thought occurs. Having a plan is like putting down the train tracks on the new neural pathway of healthy, positive thinking you are building now.

Review your entries over time to gain deeper insights into your patterns and how they affect your life.

This methodology can even help you recognize triggers in others, allowing you to remain calm amid challenging situations. For example, I noticed a recurring pattern with my spouse during a recent road trip with our three small kids. Whenever I used my phone to find a nearby place to eat, we occasionally ended up in unsafe neighborhoods. Each time this happened, my husband quickly became upset and raised his voice. Initially, I was confused by his reaction, and it even began to trigger me. However, by the second occurrence, I recognized it as a pattern. Later, during a quiet moment of reflection, I realized that he was being triggered by fear for our safety and uncertainty about his ability to protect us in potentially dangerous situations. Understanding his fear allowed me to navigate his reactions more calmly and compassionately for the rest of our trip. I didn't take his response personally; I understood he came from a place of love for us.

Setting and Maintaining Healthy Boundaries

Think of a life where you feel safe, respected, and in control of your destiny. This vision is attainable through the establishment of personal boundaries. Boundaries are the invisible lines that define where you end and others begin, a crucial framework for emotional safety and well-being. They act as a protective barrier, shielding your personal space from unwanted intrusion and maintaining the sanctity of your inner world. In relationships, boundaries serve as limits that dictate how you wish to be treated, ensuring respectful and nurturing interactions. They empower you to express your needs and desires without fear, creating a foundation for authentic and balanced connections.

To establish healthy boundaries, clear communication of your needs is critical. This requires you to articulate your limits with honesty and clarity. Begin by identifying what feels comfortable and what doesn't, then express these preferences to those around you. It might be as simple as stating, "I need some time to myself in the evenings" or "I feel uncomfortable when you speak to me that way." Assertiveness training exercises can be beneficial in this regard. These exercises teach you to speak up while maintaining respect for others confidently. Practice role-playing scenarios where you assert your boundaries, allowing you to become more comfortable with these conversations in real life. Remember, setting boundaries is not about creating walls but defining pathways for healthy interaction.

Setting boundaries can be challenging, often stirring up fears and anxieties. The fear of rejection looms large for many women, as they worry that asserting their needs might alienate loved ones. A pervasive guilt associated with saying no stems from societal conditioning that often places a higher value on pleasing others than self-care. You might find yourself agreeing to things out of obligation, even when they compromise your well-being. Overcoming these challenges requires a shift in mindset. Recognize that your needs are valid and that setting boundaries is an act of self-respect, not selfishness. Practice self-compassion by reminding yourself that boundaries are a way to honor your emotional and physical health.

Firm boundaries bring numerous benefits, enriching your relationships and personal growth. They enhance self-respect, as each boundary set reinforces the message that you value yourself and your needs. This self-respect is mirrored in how others treat you, fostering relationships built on mutual respect and understanding. Boundaries also reduce emotional exhaustion. Protecting your energy and time prevents burnout and maintains a sense of balance. This preservation allows you to engage with others from a place of fullness rather than depletion, improving the quality of your interactions. With each boundary upheld, cultivate a life reflecting your true self, where you feel empowered and in control.

Visualize the impact of boundaries like a riverbank guiding the flow of water. Without the bank, the river would scatter and lose direction.

Similarly, boundaries provide structure, guiding your life with intention and clarity. They allow you to navigate relationships, knowing your limits are respected confidently. Reflect on this: A woman who once struggled to say no to extra work found peace by setting clear boundaries with her boss. She communicated and stuck to her capacity, leading to a more balanced workload and increased job satisfaction. This change rippled into her personal life, where she could be more present with her family. Boundaries are not just about saying no; they're about saying yes to what *truly* matters.

Healing Through Relational Dynamics

Our lives are intricately woven with the threads of our relationships. Each connection, whether fleeting or enduring, has the potential to heal or harm. Relationships are mirrors, reflecting the parts of ourselves we might not readily see. In supportive relationships, we find solace and growth. These connections offer us a sanctuary where we can be vulnerable and authentic. They nurture our spirit, allowing us to explore our innermost selves without fear. However, relationships can also be toxic, draining our energy and reinforcing negative beliefs about ourselves. They can trap us in cycles of blame and resentment, mirroring the dysfunction we might have known as children. The duality of relationships means they can be our greatest source of healing and deepest source of hurt.

In the realm of relational dynamics, the **mirroring effect** is significant. We often attract individuals who reflect our unresolved issues. This phenomenon can be both illuminating and challenging. It forces us to confront the parts of ourselves we might prefer to ignore. By recognizing this mirroring, we gain insight into our emotional landscape. We see how our inner world shapes our outer experiences. This awareness is the first step in using relationships as a tool for healing. It invites us to take responsibility for our role in these dynamics and empowers us to make conscious choices about whom we allow into our lives.

Relational healing practices can transform relationships into powerful catalysts for personal growth. Open communication exercises are central to this transformation. Practicing honesty in our interactions fosters trust and intimacy. It encourages us to express our needs and boundaries clearly, creating a foundation for mutual respect. Empathy and active listening further enhance this process. By genuinely hearing another's perspective, we validate their experiences and strengthen our connection. These practices encourage us to step outside our viewpoint and consider the feelings and needs of others. They remind us that relationships are not just about receiving love and support but also about giving it.

The impact of healthy relationships on our well-being is immeasurable. They provide emotional support networks that cushion us during life's challenges. In these networks, we find allies who cheer us on and hold us accountable. They offer a space where we can process our emotions and receive guidance. Positive reinforcement of change is another gift of nurturing relationships. When those around us acknowledge our growth, it reinforces our progress and motivates us to continue. Their belief in us can bolster our self-esteem and encourage us to strive for our goals.

Here's the story of a woman who found healing through a supportive friendship. After years of toxic relationships, she met someone who saw her potential and encouraged her to pursue her dreams. This friend became a mirror, reflecting her strengths and helping her see herself in a new light. Their relationship was a haven where she could voice her fears and aspirations without judgment. Through this friendship, she learned to value herself and set boundaries with others. Her transformation was life-changing as she moved from self-doubt to empowerment. Similarly, think of couples who have grown together by embracing open communication and vulnerability. They have navigated life's challenges by supporting one another's growth and creating a resilient and nurturing partnership.

These stories illustrate the power of relational dynamics in healing. They remind us that relationships can be challenging and offer unparalleled opportunities for transformation. Engaging in healthy dynamics creates a space where healing can flourish. We invite love, empathy, and understanding into our lives, fostering connections that uplift and inspire us. This choice is a testament to our resilience and commitment to personal growth. It affirms that we deserve relationships that reflect the best of who we are.

Rewriting Your Narrative Method

We all carry stories within us, narratives that shape how we see ourselves and interact with the world. These personal narratives are powerful and can profoundly influence our mindset and behaviors. They act as the lens through which we interpret our experiences. For some, the narrative takes the form of a victim mentality, where life is viewed as a series of events happening to us, often leaving us feeling powerless and over-whelmed. This mindset can be a comforting shield, protecting us from the painful truth of unmet potential. But it can also trap us, convincing us that change is impossible and that we are forever at the mercy of our circumstances.

On the other hand, an empowered self-view transforms how we per-ceive challenges. It invites us to see ourselves as active participants in our journey, capable of affecting change and charting a new course. This shift from victimhood to empowerment is not about ignoring past wounds but writing a new chapter where healing and growth are possible.

Rewriting your narrative is a transformation exercise. It begins with the stories you tell yourself, which have been repeated for years. One effective strategy is to craft a future-focused narrative.

Interactive Exercise: Rewriting Your Narrative

Objective: Change the negative story you've been telling yourself.
Instructions:
Start by envisioning the life you want to lead and the version of your-self you aspire to be. Write this narrative in the present tense, as if it's already unfolding. Describe your strengths, your achievements, and the obstacles you've overcome. This exercise helps shift your mindset from limitation to possibility, opening the door to a future that aligns with your desires. Another crucial step is identifying and challenging limiting

beliefs that anchor you to a negative self-story. Take a moment to reflect on the beliefs that have held you back. Are they based on facts or perceptions? Challenging these beliefs requires introspection and courage, but it's vital for rewriting your narrative. Replace them with empowering truths, and over time, these new beliefs will reshape your self-perception and influence your actions.

The benefits of cultivating an empowered narrative are far-reaching. You'll likely notice an increased sense of agency as you reframe your self-story. Life no longer feels like a series of events you must endure but an adventure where you have a say. This newfound agency enhances your problem-solving abilities, allowing you to approach challenges with creativity and confidence. You become adept at navigating obstacles, viewing them as opportunities for growth rather than insurmountable barriers. With an empowered narrative, you're more resilient in the face of adversity, drawing strength from the belief that you can overcome whatever comes your way. This inner strength fosters a deep sense of self-efficacy, empowering you to pursue your goals with determination and grace.

Reflect on the stories of individuals who have successfully shifted their narratives. One woman I know grew up believing she was destined for mediocrity, a message ingrained by years of criticism. But she chose to rewrite her story, focusing on her capabilities and passions. She began volunteering in her community, eventually leading initiatives that made a tangible difference. Her narrative transformed from inadequacy to empowerment, sparking personal and professional growth. Another friend faced significant adversity after a career setback. Initially, his narrative was one of failure and defeat. Yet, he reframed his story of resilience and reinvention through intentional reflection and rewriting. He pursued new opportunities, ultimately fulfilling and succeeding in a field he never imagined. These transformations are not unique; they are testaments to the power of narrative. They remind us that while we can't always control our circumstances, we can choose how we interpret and respond to them. The narrative we embrace becomes the foundation on which we build our lives, inviting us to step into a story of empowerment and possibility.

The Cycle of Self-Sabotage: Breaking Free

Self-sabotage is a perplexing dance between desire and fear, often playing out in the most subtle ways. It's the internal tug-of-war where you might sincerely wish for success yet unconsciously set up barriers that prevent you from achieving it. This behavior manifests in various forms, such as procrastination, delaying tasks to the point of crisis or avoidance, and sidestepping opportunities because they feel too daunting. Self-limiting behaviors are another hallmark, where you might convince yourself you're incapable or undeserving of the success you seek. These manifestations of self-sabotage are rooted in deeply ingrained beliefs often formed during childhood, where experiences taught you that safety lies in staying small or unseen. They create a cycle that can be difficult to break, as each act of sabotage reinforces the belief that you're not enough.

Recognizing when engaging in self-sabotage is the first step toward breaking free from its grip. This process begins with self-reflection, where you ask yourself questions that delve into the heart of your actions. Contemplate queries like, "What am I avoiding right now?" or "Why do I feel unworthy of my goals?" These questions can illuminate patterns that have been operating under the surface. Identifying these patterns of avoidance is crucial. You may notice a tendency to seek distractions when faced with challenging tasks or an impulse to downplay your achievements in conversations. By bringing these behaviors into the light, you can begin to understand their origins and motivations. This awareness is empowering, as it lays the groundwork for meaningful change.

Actionable strategies are essential to overcoming self-sabotage. Setting realistic goals is a powerful approach. Begin by breaking down larger objectives into smaller, manageable tasks. This step-by-step process reduces overwhelm and provides a clear path forward, allowing you to experience achievement. Building accountability partnerships can also be transformative. Find someone you trust—whether a friend, family member, or mentor—who can hold you accountable for your goals. Share your aspirations and challenges with them, and establish regular check-ins to discuss progress. This external support reinforces your commitment and offers encouragement during moments of doubt. It creates a shared investment in your success, making it harder to revert to self-sabotaging behaviors.

The benefits of overcoming self-sabotage touch every aspect of your life. As you dismantle these destructive patterns, you pave the way for personal growth and success. Greater confidence naturally follows as each step forward reinforces your belief in your capabilities. This newfound self-esteem becomes a sturdy foundation, allowing you to approach challenges with assurance and resilience. Achieving personal goals that once felt out of reach becomes possible. The barriers that once seemed impossible begin to crumble, replaced by a sense of empowerment and possibility. This transformation is about achieving external success and nurturing an inner narrative of worthiness and potential. It's about reclaiming your power and stepping into a life where self-doubt no longer holds you back.

Transforming Fear Into Empowerment

Fear is a curious thing. It sits quietly in the corners of our minds, whispering doubts and weaving stories that keep us tethered to the *familiar*. It often masquerades as a protector, warning us of the dangers beyond our comfort zones. Yet, beneath this guise, fear can become a formidable barrier to change, holding us captive within negative cycles. It is the fear of failure that often looms largest, casting a shadow over our dreams and aspirations. This fear convinces us that mistakes reflect our worth rather than stepping stones to growth. Equally paralyzing is the fear of the unknown, the vast expanse of possibilities that excite and intimidate us. This fear invites us to stay put, to cling to the certainty of what we know, even if it no longer serves us.

But what if we could transform fear into a source of empowerment? What if we could reframe it as a catalyst for growth rather than a stumbling block? Visualization exercises offer a powerful tool for doing just that. Picture your success in vivid detail, engaging all your senses to create a compelling mental image of what you wish to achieve. See yourself navigating challenges with confidence and overcoming obstacles with ease. This practice bolsters your belief in your capabilities and diminishes the power of fear by focusing your mind on positive outcomes. Courage-building practices further this transformation by encouraging you to take small, calculated risks. Start with manageable challenges that stretch your comfort zone, gradually building your tolerance for uncertainty. Each step forward, no matter how small, reinforces your resilience and fortifies your courage.

The benefits of embracing fear are manifold, extending far beyond the initial discomfort. You cultivate increased resilience and adaptability as you face and transform your fears. You become more adept at navigating life's uncertainties, viewing them as opportunities for growth rather than threats to your security. This adaptability enhances your ability to respond to change gracefully and confidently, empowering you to embrace new experiences with an open heart. Moreover, as you confront your fears, your self-confidence grows. You begin to see yourself as capable and resourceful, dismantling the limiting beliefs that once held you back. This newfound confidence is a powerful motivator, propelling you toward your goals with renewed vigor.

Bear in mind the stories of individuals who have turned their fears into driving forces for positive change. Take, for example, the woman who once struggled with crippling anxiety. Her fear of public speaking was so intense that it threatened her career. But rather than succumbing to this fear, she faced it head-on. She enrolled in a public speaking course, practicing in front of supportive peers who encouraged her every step of the way. Over time, her anxiety transformed into a sense of accomplishment as she delivered presentations with poise and clarity. Her story is a testament to the power of facing fears, demonstrating how they can evolve from obstacles into stepping stones.

Another example is a dear friend who used her fear of failure as a springboard for personal growth. After a series of setbacks, she realized that her fear prevented her from pursuing her passion for writing. Instead of letting this fear dictate her actions, she reframed it as a challenge to be met. She began writing daily, embracing the vulnerability of sharing her work with others. This practice honed her craft and instilled a deep sense of fulfillment and purpose. Her journey illustrates how fear, when acknowledged and embraced, can lead to lasting transformation and empowerment.

As we conclude this chapter, remember that fear does not define you. It is a natural part of the human experience, a signal that you are on the brink of something new. By facing your fears, you unlock the potential for growth and empowerment, paving the way for a life rich with possibility. Embrace fear as a companion on your path, knowing that the seeds of your greatest strength lie within its depths. You can transform fear into a force for positive change, shaping a future where you can pursue your dreams with courage and confidence.

CHAPTER SIX

INNER CHILD LINKED TO PARENTING AND GENERATIONAL HEALING

"Your inner child carries the unresolved pain of generations. Healing it creates a ripple effect." Catherine Ingram

It was a crisp autumn morning when I found myself saying something to my daughter about her outfit that I swore I'd never say. A phrase passed down like a family heirloom slipped out of my mouth before I could catch it. I realized I was not just a parent but a link in a chain of generational patterns, some of which I wanted desperately to break. This awareness is the first step in understanding the generational cycle of trauma—a cycle that can unconsciously imprint itself on family dynamics, shaping how we relate to one another.

Even if you're not a parent, this chapter will bring insights into how your parents might have raised you. All parents have been repeating unconscious behaviors from past generations, and it's a blessing for us to understand *how* this generational trauma works to have more compassion toward them and our inner child.

Generational trauma is a complex web woven through our family histories, passed down like the stories we tell at gatherings. It is not just the memories of past experiences but also the emotional imprints they leave behind. This trauma can manifest in ways both subtle and profound, influencing how we interact with our children and each other. Research in epigenetics suggests that trauma can affect gene expression, altering how our bodies respond to stress and emotion. This means that the echoes of past trauma can be present *even* in those who never directly experienced it. Our ancestors' struggles can become our own, not because we choose them, but because they are etched into the very fabric of our being.

One of the most famous scientific experiments in epigenetics proves this point with experiments involving mice and cherry blossoms. In this experiment, researchers exposed mice to a specific scent (cherry blossoms) while simultaneously giving them a mild electric shock. The mice developed a fear response to the smell alone. When these mice later had offspring, the next generation *also* exhibited a fear response to the scent, even without direct exposure to the trauma.

This study demonstrated that the trauma experienced by the parent mice altered gene expression through epigenetic changes, which were then passed on to their descendants. This suggests that experiences and traumas can impact not just the individual but also their offspring, linking it to the concept of generational trauma in humans.

One of the most insidious aspects of generational trauma is the way it perpetuates itself through learned behaviors and coping mechanisms. We often inherit patterns of communication, conflict, and emotional expression from our parents, who inherited them from their parents. Carl Jung's concept of "projection" provides insight into this phenomenon. *We might project our unresolved issues onto our children, treating them in ways that mirror how we were treated at that young age.* This cycle can continue unchecked until we become conscious of it and make a deliberate effort to change.

Recognizing the signs of generational trauma is crucial for any parent looking to break free from its grip. Recurring family conflicts that arise out of nowhere may be rooted in unresolved issues passed down through generations. You might use the **exact phrases** or **discipline techniques** as your parents, even if they didn't serve you well. Patterns of emotional suppression, where family members avoid discussing feelings or addressing conflict, can also indicate generational trauma. These are harmless quirks and indicators of more profound, inherited wounds that need addressing.

The impact of generational trauma on children can be far-reaching, affecting their emotional development in ways both visible and hidden. Children growing up in families with unresolved trauma may experience anxiety and attachment issues, struggling to form secure bonds with others. They might display behavioral problems in school, acting out to express the emotions they cannot articulate. These children carry the weight of past generations, often without understanding why. It's a heavy burden that can shape their sense of self and future relationships.

Breaking the cycle of generational trauma requires intention and effort. As parents, we play a pivotal role in disrupting these patterns for future generations. Conscious parenting practices, which involve being aware of our actions and reactions, can help us recognize when we are perpetuating old cycles. Addressing *our* inner child wounds and healing ourselves is critical to breaking this generational cycle of abuse. The inner work you are doing right now with this book will enable you to parent from a place of awareness and empathy rather than reaction. By doing this work, we free ourselves and pave the way for our children to grow up without the shadows of the past dictating their lives.

Reflective Exercise: Identifying Generational Patterns

Objective: Increase awareness of generational patterns in your family.
  Instructions:

1. **List common phrases**. Write down phrases or sayings often used in your family. Examples: "Boys don't cry!" "Stop being such a drama queen," and "Girls don't look pretty when they are angry." Reflect on their origin and impact.

2. **Map family conflicts.** Identify recurring conflicts or negative behaviors in your family. Example: Screaming at the top of your lungs to your toddler or forcing someone to hug another family member when they don't want to. Think about their roots and any patterns.

3. **Reflect on emotional expression.** Note how your family expresses or suppresses emotions. What positive or harmful coping mechanisms did you observe growing up? Take note of how these patterns affect you and your children.

Reflect on these patterns and consider steps you might take to alter them, paving the way for healthier family dynamics.

Parenting With Awareness and Empathy

Imagine a scene where your child approaches you with a problem, their eyes wide with anticipation. In that moment, mindful parenting invites you to pause, let go of distractions, and offer your *entire* presence. Being aware and empathetic in your parenting transforms interactions into opportunities for connection. It's about actively listening—not just hearing words, but truly understanding the emotions behind them. This goes beyond surface-level exchanges, encouraging a deeper bond between you and your child. When you engage in empathetic communication, you create a space where your child feels valued and understood. It's a practice of seeing the world through their eyes, acknowledging their experiences as valid, and responding with kindness and patience.

Think about incorporating **reflective listening exercises** into your daily interactions to cultivate empathy in your parenting. Begin by paraphrasing what your child says and reflecting on it with empathy. This not only ensures you understand their perspective but also validates their feelings. For instance, if your child expresses frustration about a tough day at school, you might respond, "It sounds like today was challenging for you, and that must have been tough." This simple act of acknowledgment can soothe emotional wounds and foster trust. Emotional validation practices further strengthen this bond. When your child shares their feelings, resist the urge to solve the problem immediately. Instead, recognize their emotions, letting them know it's okay to feel what they feel. This approach empowers your child to process feelings healthily, building confidence and emotional intelligence.

The benefits of empathetic parenting are vast, creating a foundation of security and trust that permeates your child's life. As you practice empathy, you weave threads of connection between you and your child, strengthening emotional bonds that withstand the tests of time. This connection fosters a sense of safety, allowing your child to confidently explore the world, knowing they have a secure base to return to. With this security, children are more likely to develop self-assurance and resilience, facing challenges with courage and adaptability. They learn that their feelings are valid and that they can navigate life's highs and lows. Empathetic parenting builds a bridge for open communication, inviting your child to share their thoughts and emotions.

Yet, maintaining empathy in parenting has its challenges. The demands of daily life, coupled with personal stress and frustration, can make it difficult to remain patient and empathetic. It's crucial to recognize these challenges and address them with intention. Managing parental stress involves setting aside time for **self-care**, ensuring you recharge and nurture your well-being. This might include mindfulness practices, exercise, or taking a few moments of solitude. I like to say, "You can't give from an empty cup." Caring for yourself creates the capacity to be present and empathetic with your child. Balancing empathy with discipline is another aspect of this practice. While empathy involves understanding and validating emotions, it doesn't mean forgoing boundaries or expectations. Instead, approach discipline with empathy, explaining the reasons behind rules and consequences. This reinforces that discipline stems from love and a desire to guide rather than control.

In this mindful parenting journey, remember that perfection is *not* the goal. It's about progress and the willingness to learn and grow alongside your child. Each moment of connection, each empathetic exchange, contributes to a tapestry of love and understanding that shapes your child's world. Through awareness and empathy, you offer your child the gift of being seen, heard, and cherished, laying the groundwork for a lifetime of secure, trusting relationships.

Healing Your Inner Child to Heal Your Children

The connection between healing your inner child and effective parenting is powerful. Addressing your childhood wounds allows you to release the weight of past emotional baggage, freeing you to be fully present with your children. As you work through these unresolved issues, you model healthy emotional behavior, demonstrating resilience and vulnerability. This authentic way of being teaches your children invaluable lessons about self-acceptance and emotional regulation. By healing yourself, you create a home environment rooted in stability and understanding rather than the echoes of past trauma. This shift enriches your relationship with your children and fosters a culture of open expression and mutual respect.

The benefits of parents addressing their trauma extend beyond personal growth. Children thrive in environments where parents model emotional health, witnessing firsthand the power of self-awareness and healing. When you heal, familial tensions often diminish, replaced by an atmosphere of understanding and empathy. Children learn to express themselves openly, knowing they will be met with compassion rather than judgment. This healthier emotional modeling nurtures their self-confidence and determinism, helping them develop a strong sense of self. As a parent who has healed, you avoid the unpredictable shifts between calm and chaos, providing a stable foundation for your children to build upon.

It's essential to remember that children learn not by being told what to do but by copying what the adults in their lives do. When healing your inner child, you have much more empathy, compassion, and patience. Your children learn how to be from your *actions*. A calm mother can parent in an easier way than a frantic one. Children will also learn how to address triggering situations by observing how their parents respond or react—similar to the phrase "monkey see, monkey do." Your *role modeling* is one of the main ways children learn how to think, talk, and behave.

Countless stories illustrate the transformative power of inner child healing in parents. One mother, who struggled with anger and anxiety, found solace in addressing her childhood traumas. She learned to release her past through journaling and mindfulness, creating a harmonious relationship with her children. Once filled with tension, her home became a sanctuary of love and support. Another father, haunted by memories of neglect, turned to visualization techniques to heal his inner child. As he embraced his past, he discovered a newfound ability to connect with his children, fostering a bond built on trust and understanding. These stories serve as beacons of hope, illustrating that healing is possible and paving the way for healthier, more connected families.

Emotional Intelligence for Parents

Emotional intelligence in parenting is about more than just managing one's own emotions; it's about understanding and nurturing the emotional landscape of your entire family. Emotional intelligence involves self-awareness in parenting decisions, allowing you to recognize how emotions influence your interactions with your children. It's about regulating your emotions during parent-child interactions, ensuring your responses are thoughtful rather than reactive. This awareness is crucial because it sets the tone for how your children perceive and manage their emotions. When you approach parenting with emotional intelligence, you create a model for your children, teaching them the importance of understanding their feelings and those of others. This approach fosters an environment where emotions are acknowledged and respected, laying the groundwork for healthy emotional development.

Developing emotional intelligence is a skill that can be honed with intentional practice. Start by engaging in emotional self-assessment, a reflective exercise encouraging you to examine your emotional triggers and responses. By identifying the situations that provoke strong emotions, you can better prepare to handle them calmly and constructively. Keep a journal where you note these instances, reflecting on your feelings and why. This practice cultivates a deeper understanding of your emotional patterns, empowering you to make conscious choices in your interactions. Teaching emotional vocabulary to your children is another powerful tool. Encourage them to articulate their feelings by introducing words that describe a range of emotions. Simple exercises, such as asking them to describe their feelings and why, can enhance their emotional literacy, enabling them to communicate their needs more effectively.

The influence of emotionally intelligent parenting on family dynamics is substantial. Parents who practice emotional intelligence often find conflicts resolved more efficiently and amicably. You create space for dialogue and understanding when you approach disagreements with empathy and an open mind. This approach diffuses tension and strengthens the bonds between family members. Enhanced family communication is another benefit, as emotionally intelligent parents foster an atmosphere where every member feels heard and valued. It's critical here to listen intently to the child's telling of events, especially if they made a mistake or behaved negatively. More often than not, children want to do something good, but their actions fall short. As emotionally intelligent parents, we must listen to and understand what the child is trying to accomplish. This open communication builds trust and respect, encouraging children to express themselves without fear of judgment or dismissal. As a result, children learn to navigate social relationships with confidence and empathy, skills that serve them well throughout their lives.

Take into account the story of a family who transformed their interactions through the application of emotional intelligence. A mother struggling with balancing work and family life decided to focus on developing her emotional intelligence. She began practicing mindfulness, taking a few moments each day to center herself before engaging with her children. This simple shift allowed her to approach parenting with a sense of calm and clarity. Over time, she noticed a significant change in her family dynamics. Her children became more open and communicative, sharing their thoughts and feelings more easily. Conflicts that once escalated quickly were now resolved with understanding and cooperation. This transformation extended beyond the home, as her children demonstrated increased empathy and emotional resilience in their interactions with peers and teachers.

Here's another example of an emotionally intelligent mother. A mother received an email from her child's teacher, upset over her eight-year-old's disrespectful comment. Instead of reacting angrily, she calmly asked her child to explain what happened. The child revealed he had repeated a phrase he'd heard from older kids, aiming to make others laugh, not realizing it had a negative connotation. The mother recognized his good intentions (in this case, wanting to make others laugh) and explained why his behavior didn't match his goal. With this understanding, he didn't repeat the mistake. She helped him make amends by writing his teacher a letter of apology. Had the mother reacted harshly, he might have felt misunderstood, risking their connection. When children feel seen and heard, they trust us, and we can be more open to sharing our lessons.

Successful parent-child collaborations offer further testimony to the power of emotional intelligence. One father, keenly aware of his daughter's struggles with anxiety, implemented regular family meetings where emotions were discussed openly. He encouraged each family member to share the highs and lows of the week, fostering a sense of connection and support. This practice not only deepened their understanding of each other's experiences but also equipped his daughter with the tools to manage her anxiety more effectively. The family meetings became a cherished ritual, a time to connect and reflect, strengthening their bonds and nurturing their emotional well-being. These stories illustrate that emotionally intelligent parenting is not about achieving perfection but creating a nurturing environment where every emotion is given a voice and valued for its insight.

Creating a Nurturing Environment

Imagine your home as a sanctuary where your children feel love and security. This environment provides the foundation for their growth, a nurturing space where they can explore, learn, and express themselves freely. Critical components of such an environment include emotional safety and security, where children feel accepted and loved for who they are. This begins with creating a space where their feelings are acknowledged and respected, fostering a sense of trust. Consistent routines and boundaries reinforce this safety, offering structure and predictability that help children understand their world. Children who know what to expect feel more secure, allowing them to navigate life's challenges confidently.

To cultivate a nurturing atmosphere, think about engaging in family rituals and traditions that strengthen bonds and create lasting memories. Whether a weekly game night or a simple bedtime routine, these rituals provide moments of connection and joy. They offer opportunities for family members to come together, share experiences, and celebrate each other. Encouraging open communication is equally important.

Foster an environment where *everyone* feels comfortable expressing their thoughts and emotions. This might involve setting aside time for family discussions or creating a safe space where children can share their feelings without fear of judgment. By prioritizing communication, you demonstrate that every voice matters, reinforcing that home is a place of support and understanding.

The impact of a nurturing environment on children's emotional and psychological development is impactful. When children feel secure, their self-esteem flourishes. They develop a sense of autonomy and confidence when making decisions and solving problems. This confidence extends to their learning and creativity, as they feel empowered to explore new ideas and take risks. In a supportive environment, children are encouraged to ask questions, express curiosity, and pursue their passions. This atmosphere nurtures their creativity, allowing them to think outside the box and approach challenges with a growth mindset. As a result, they develop the skills and resilience needed to thrive in an ever-changing world.

Consider a family who transformed their home into a nurturing haven. Once a place of chaos and stress, their home became a sanctuary of calm and connection. They started by establishing a daily gratitude ritual, where each family member shared something they were thankful for. This simple practice shifted the focus from conflict to appreciation, fostering a positive atmosphere. They also implemented a family meeting once a week, where everyone could discuss their thoughts and feelings openly. This practice encouraged communication and understanding, strengthening their bonds and creating a sense of unity. Over time, the family noticed significant changes. The children became more confident and engaged, eager to share their ideas and explore their interests. Once filled with tension, their home now resonated with laughter and love.

In another example, a family introduced a monthly "creativity day," where they dedicated a day to exploring new activities together. They embraced learning and creating as a team, whether painting, building, or cooking. This tradition became a cherished part of their lives, providing a space for self-expression and collaboration. The children thrived in this environment, developing their creative skills and ability to work together and support each other. These stories illustrate the transformative power of a nurturing home where love, communication, and creativity flourish.

The Power of Apology and Forgiveness in Families

Apology and forgiveness are like the gentle balm that soothes the inevitable bruises of family life. They are powerful practices that mend the small and large rifts in the intimate dance of living with others. In a family where emotions run deep, and interactions are frequent, the capacity to apologize sincerely and forgive wholeheartedly can determine the health of relationships. These practices are not just about apologizing or letting go; they are about repairing emotional harm and building a foundation of mutual respect and understanding. Apologies, when genuine, acknowledge the hurt caused and take responsibility for actions. This act of humility and empathy can repair bonds that might otherwise fray. Forgiveness, on the other hand, is an act of release. It frees both the forgiver and the forgiven from the chains of resentment and past grievances. These practices create a dynamic where love and understanding prevail over discord and distance.

Specific techniques can be employed to practice effective apology and forgiveness with certain family members. A sincere acknowledgment of mistakes is the cornerstone of an effective apology. This means going beyond a cursory "I'm sorry" and articulating the specific behavior or action that caused harm. It involves expressing genuine remorse and a willingness to make amends. Equally important is the expression of empathy and understanding. Letting the other person know that you comprehend the impact of your actions on their feelings can bridge the gap created by the conflict. Forgiveness requires a conscious decision to let go of resentment and to cease holding past mistakes over someone's head. Regular family discussions about feelings and conflicts can facilitate a culture of openness and forgiveness, where issues are addressed before they become more significant problems.

The benefits of apology and forgiveness in a family are transformative. Conflicts and tensions are naturally reduced when sincere apologies are offered and accepted. This reduced discord creates a more harmonious environment where family members feel safe and valued. Increased empathy and compassion often follow as family members learn to see each other as fallible yet lovable. This empathy fosters deeper connections, where each person feels understood and supported. The emotional resilience of a family strengthens as well. When conflict arises, knowing that reconciliation is possible and that love is resilient in the face of mistakes provides a solid foundation for weathering future challenges.

Ponder the story of the Johnson family, who found themselves locked in a cycle of blame and misunderstanding. Arguments would escalate quickly, leaving emotional scars long after apologies were mumbled. It wasn't until they began practicing sincere apology and forgiveness that their dynamics shifted. By acknowledging their mistakes openly and expressing empathy, they were able to heal past wounds. The Johnsons emerged from this process with stronger bonds and a renewed sense of connection. Their story illustrates the healing power of these practices, demonstrating that reconciliation is possible even in the most strained relationships.

In another example, a mother shares her testimonial with us. She and her daughter had drifted apart due to years of unresolved conflict. They began to communicate openly by writing letters with open hearts, apologizing, and forgiving past grievances. This process wasn't easy, but it allowed them to rebuild their relationship on a foundation of trust and mutual respect. Their story serves as a testament to the transformative power of apology and forgiveness, highlighting how these practices can bridge the gaps that life inevitably creates.

This example highlights the importance of closing the emotional cycle. A mother and father had a heated argument at the dinner table in front of their two children. They excused themselves to cool off and later forgave each other. Realizing the children hadn't seen this reconciliation, the mother and father went to where their children were playing, re-enacting their apologies. By showing forgiveness, they demonstrated to their children how conflict can be resolved, allowing them to witness the complete cycle of forgiveness.

As we conclude this chapter, we've explored the intricate layers of parenting and family dynamics, from understanding generational cycles to the transformative power of apology. Moving forward, we'll delve into holistic healing approaches, where body, mind, and spirit unite to pursue well-being.

CHAPTER SEVEN

HOLISTIC HEALING FOR INNER CHILD INTEGRATION

"To heal, we must integrate all aspects of our being—mind, body, and spirit." Louise Hay

Imagine sitting quietly, breathing so deeply that it feels as though the world pauses for just a moment. In that breath, there is a sense of release, a quiet invitation to let go of the tensions that cling to your shoulders and mind. This moment of stillness is not just a pause; it's a gateway to healing. Meditation and breathwork are potent tools for calming the mind and nurturing inner peace, offering sanctuary amid chaos. They invite you to explore the depths of your being with gentle curiosity, transforming stress and anxiety into clarity and focus.

Meditation lets you retreat from the whirlwind of thoughts and emotions, creating space for peace and understanding. By developing focus and concentration, meditation is a balm for the restless mind, offering moments of clarity amid the noise. This practice strengthens the prefrontal cortex and hippocampus, counteracting the effects of trauma by reducing hyperactivity in the amygdala, as research highlights. Sitting in silence, observing your thoughts without judgment, fosters a meaningful sense of calm and balance. Over time, this practice can transform your relationship with stress, allowing you to navigate life's challenges with grace and resilience.

Several meditation practices are available, each offering unique benefits. Guided meditations designed explicitly for inner child healing can be potent. These meditations gently guide you through visualizations and affirmations, helping you connect with your inner child in a safe, nurturing space. Remember, you have free access to download the audio to your phone so you can do the guided meditations:

Or go to the website https://www.michelleduffy1111.com/audiosfo rhealingyourinnerchildbook

Mindfulness meditation, on the other hand, invites you to be present in the moment, observing your thoughts and bodily sensations with compassionate awareness. This practice cultivates a sense of presence, teaching you to respond to life's fluctuations with calmness and understanding.

Establishing a consistent meditation practice requires intention and commitment. Creating a dedicated meditation space in your home can anchor this practice, offering a physical reminder of your commitment to self-care. This space might include a comfortable cushion, calming scents, or meaningful objects that inspire tranquility. Setting achievable meditation goals is also crucial. Start with a few minutes each day, gradually increasing the duration as you become more comfortable with the practice. Remember, meditation is not about perfection but presence. Approach each session with an open heart and mind, allowing yourself to be exactly as you are now.

Interactive Exercise: Building Your Meditation Practice

Objective: Establish a consistent meditation practice to support emotional well-being.

Instructions:

1. **Create your space.** Choose a peaceful corner in your home and personalize it with cushions, candles, or calming scents. Sit down crossed-legged or in a chair.

2. **Set your schedule.** Decide a regular time for your practice, whether morning or evening and commit to it.

3. **Start small.** Begin with 5 minutes a day, focusing on your breath and gradually increasing the time as you grow comfortable.

4. **Reflect.** Keep a record of your experiences, challenges, and insights gained through your practice.

Breathwork complements meditation by offering tangible techniques to release emotional tension and stress. **Deep diaphragmatic breathing** is a foundational practice where you engage your diaphragm to take full, deep breaths. This technique soothes the nervous system, promoting relaxation and emotional release. **Box breathing**, another effective method, involves inhaling, holding the breath, exhaling, and holding again for equal counts. This structured breathing pattern helps regulate the breath and calm the mind, especially during heightened anxiety. **Transformational Breathwork**, a more intensive practice, employs conscious breathing patterns to access deep emotional layers. This technique is best explored with a Certified Coach like myself to ensure a safe and supportive experience.

Interactive Exercise: Deep Diaphragmatic Breathing

Objective: Using this breathing technique to release stress and increase lung expansion.

Instructions:

1. **Get comfortable.** This breathing is best done on a yoga mat or blanket. Lay down on your back.

2. **Process.** Place one hand on your belly and another on your

chest. When you inhale, focus on your belly so that it rises, and then, on your exhalation, let your belly fall flat. Breathe in through your nose and exhale through your nose or mouth slowly.

This movement is innate in babies if you see them lying on their backs. Their belly automatically rises in the inhale and falls in the exhale. Unfortunately, many adults have lost this way of breathing, but practicing this helps us regain this way and increases the oxygen capacity we take in. Notice that at the beginning of this practice, you might only be able to inhale very shallowly. Still, with practice and time, your inhalation can inflate your belly and expand to your shoulders for maximum lung expansion.

3. Set a routine. Begin with 1 minute a day, focusing on your breath, and gradually increase the time as you grow comfortable, up to 5 minutes.

4. Reflect. Keep notes of your experiences, challenges, and insights gained through your practice.

Interactive Exercise: Box Breathing or Four Square Breathing

Objective: Using this breathing technique to release stress and have focus and calm.

Instructions:

1. **Get comfortable.** Find a place to lie on a mat or sit on a chair.

2. **Set your schedule.** Decide a regular time for your practice,

whether morning or evening and commit to it.

3. **Process.** Inhale through your nose for 4 seconds, hold for 4 seconds, exhale through your mouth for 4 seconds, and pause for 4 seconds. Then, repeat the cycle.

4. **Start small.** Start with 1 minute a day, focusing on your breath, and gradually increase the time as you grow comfortable, up to 5 minutes daily.

5. **Reflect.** Keep a list of your experiences, challenges, and insights gained through your practice.

As you embark on this journey of meditation and breathwork, nurture yourself with patience and compassion. These practices offer a path to deeper self-awareness and healing, inviting you to explore the rich landscape of your inner world with curiosity and grace.

Healing Through Movement and Dance

Envision a day when your body feels like a vessel of unexpressed energy, yearning for release. Movement and dance become your refuge, offering a pathway to express emotions that words cannot capture. This form of expression is not just about physical activity; it's an emotional outlet that allows you to release pent-up emotions and connect deeply with your inner self. Movement is a language of the body, speaking the truths held within. When you dance, you access a freedom that transcends the confines of everyday life, tapping into a wellspring of joy, sorrow, and everything in between.

The therapeutic benefits of movement are powerful, as it bridges the gap between physical sensation and emotional release. When you move through dance, yoga, or other forms of exercise, you engage the body and mind in a harmonious dance of healing. This connection allows you to process emotions stored within the body, facilitating a cathartic and liberating release. The rhythmic nature of movement, especially in dance, activates this emotional release, freeing you from the burdens that weigh you down. It becomes a meditative practice in its own right, allowing you to reconnect with your body and emotions safely and expressively.

There are many healing movements to explore, each offering unique paths to emotional release and relaxation. **Rhythmic dancing,** for instance, is an excellent way to let go of inhibitions and express yourself freely. It can be as simple as swaying to your favorite music or joining a dance class where you can lose yourself in the rhythm. Gentle **yoga,** or **qigong,** on the other hand, focuses on mindful movements and breathing, promoting relaxation and inner calm. These practices emphasize the mind-body connection, helping you cultivate peace and balance. Engaging in these movements allows you to experience a profound sense of release and rejuvenation.

Creating a personal movement practice tailored to your needs can enhance emotional healing significantly. Begin by setting intentions for each session. This could be as simple as focusing on releasing stress or embracing joy. Intentions guide your practice, giving it purpose and direction. As you explore different movement styles, reflect on what feels right for you. Some days, a vigorous dance session might be what you need; other times, gentle stretches might speak to your soul. Listen to your body and allow it to guide you to the movement that resonates most deeply. This practice becomes an intimate dialogue between you and your inner self, fostering healing and connection.

Incorporating movement into daily life doesn't require grand gestures. Small, intentional actions can make a significant impact. Take short dance breaks during work to shake off the stress and refocus. These movement moments can refresh your mind and body, increasing productivity and creativity. Another simple practice is a **morning stretching ritual**, where you greet the day with mindful stretches. This ritual awakens your body and sets a positive tone for the hours ahead. By weaving movement into your daily routine, you create opportunities for healing and expression, nurturing your well-being in subtle yet powerful ways.

Interactive Exercise: Designing Your Movement Practice

Objective: Create a personalized movement routine to support emotional healing.

Instructions:

1. **Set your intention.** Decide what you want to focus on during your movement session, such as stress release or joy.

2. **Choose your style.** Explore different types of movement—dance, yoga, or qigong—and select what resonates with you.

3. **Schedule your sessions.** Dedicate specific times for movement

in your day, whether a morning stretch or a dance break.

4. **Reflect and adjust.** Keep a journal to note how each session makes you feel and adjust your practice as needed.

Movement and dance offer a sanctuary for expression and healing, providing a foundation for emotional release and connection. These practices invite you to embrace your body and emotions openly and acceptably, fostering a sense of freedom and vitality.

Vagus Nerve Stimulation to Reduce Stress

The vagus nerve, often described as a communication highway between your brain and body, is pivotal in your overall calm and well-being. It is a critical component of the parasympathetic nervous system and is responsible for the body's rest-and-digest functions. When this nerve is stimulated, it sends signals that promote relaxation and reduce stress. Its influence extends to mood regulation, offering relief from symptoms of depression and anxiety. Additionally, the vagus nerve's role in reducing symptoms of PTSD and trauma can be impactful, providing a natural pathway to emotional stability. By engaging the vagus nerve, you tap into a powerful mechanism for healing that aligns the mind and body in harmony.

There are simple yet effective techniques for stimulating the vagus nerve that you can incorporate into your daily life. **Humming** or **chant-**

ing is one such method. The vibrations produced by humming gently stimulate the vagus nerve, creating a sense of calm and safety. It's a practice that can be done anywhere, serving as a quick tool to soothe an anxious mind. Next time you feel overwhelmed, try humming softly to yourself. Observe how the gentle vibrations resonate through your body, fostering a sense of peace. Chanting works similarly, with the added benefit of engaging your breath and voice in a rhythmic pattern that enhances relaxation.

Interactive Element: Humming Using the Word "Aum" (om)

Objective: Stimulate the vagus nerve by humming to self-regulate your nervous system and promote overall well-being.

Instructions: You can use different words to hum. I like to use "om," which is pronounced "aum," which is considered the sound of the universe.

1. **Find a calm environment.** It promotes peace and relaxation.

2. **Get into a comfortable position.** Sit or lie down. Close your eyes if you feel like it.

3. **Hum.** Take a deep inhale through your nose, and on the exhale with your mouth closed, hum the word aaaaaauuuuuuuuuuum-mmmmmmm.

4. **Focus on the sound.** Sense the vibration within your body.

Notice the vibration in your mouth, throat, and chest.

5. **Rest and repeat.** Do this for about 10 or 15 times.

Another accessible technique is **gargling with water**. This might sound simple, but gargling stimulates the muscles in the throat, activating the vagus nerve. Consider incorporating this practice into your morning routine or whenever you need to reset. As you gargle, focus on the sensation in your throat and the sound of the water. It's a small ritual that can have a significant impact, helping to shift your body from a state of stress to one of relaxation. These techniques, although straightforward, offer powerful support in managing stress and emotional tension.

For those seeking a deeper engagement with the vagus nerve, exploring more structured practices under the guidance of a professional might be worthwhile. Techniques like Transformative Breathwork, which involves specific breathing patterns, can intensively activate the vagus nerve and support emotional release. Working with a Certified Coach ensures you approach these practices safely, maximizing their benefits and minimizing risks. The guidance of a professional can offer personalized insights, helping you tailor these practices to your unique needs and experiences.

The benefits of stimulating the vagus nerve extend beyond immediate stress relief. Regularly engaging this nerve can improve your overall mood and enhance your resilience to life's challenges. The calming effect on the nervous system supports recovery from stress and trauma, promoting balance and well-being. As you integrate these practices into your life, notice how they influence your emotional landscape. You might find that moments of stress become less overwhelming, replaced by a sense of calm that arises naturally and effortlessly. This shift is not just about managing stress at the moment; it's about cultivating a deeper understanding of peace and stability that permeates your daily life.

Incorporating vagus nerve stimulation into your routine is a testament to the power of simple practices. It's about finding moments in your day to connect with your body's innate wisdom and using these techniques to nurture and support yourself. You engage with a fundamental part of your body's healing potential through humming, gargling, or guided practices. This approach invites you to listen to your body and respond with care and intention, fostering a relationship with yourself rooted in compassion and understanding.

Spiritual Practices for Inner Peace

In the quiet moments of introspection, spirituality extends a hand, offering solace and understanding. For many women navigating the complexities of life, spiritual practices provide a path to emotional peace and resilience. Spirituality allows you to explore the deeper meanings behind experiences, offering a sense of purpose that transcends the daily grind. It's about connecting with something larger than yourself, whether that's a divine presence, nature, or the interconnectedness of humanity. This search for meaning and connection can anchor you amid life's storms and infuse your journey with hope and clarity.

Spiritual practices can be woven into the fabric of your healing approach, each offering unique ways to connect with the divine or sacred. Prayer is a practice of speaking from the heart, whether in gratitude or in seeking guidance. It can be a moment of vulnerability where you express your innermost thoughts to a higher power. Rituals and ceremonies, on the other hand, provide structure and symbolism. Lighting a candle or performing a simple ceremony can mark transitions, set intentions, or celebrate milestones. These acts of reverence invite you to pause and reflect, creating sacred moments in the everyday. Nature-based spirituality, too, holds lasting potential for healing. Spending time in nature, whether walking through a forest or sitting by the ocean, fosters a sense of connection with the natural world. It reminds you of your place within the larger tapestry of life, nurturing a sense of belonging and peace.

Spirituality and religion are distinct concepts. You can be both religious and spiritual, or spiritual, without following a specific religion. Spirituality deepens our connection to our true self—the unconditional love we naturally embody. This is the focus of my work with clients after they have addressed inner issues related to mind and body. Once subconscious limiting beliefs and inner child wounds are healed, it becomes easier to work on the soul. Soul work involves self-realization practices that cultivate deeper levels of compassion, clarify your life purpose, and heighten intuition. This journey fosters a deep sense of belonging, fulfillment, and inner peace, independent of external circumstances. It's meaningful inner work that brings rewarding, much-needed healing to our world.

Engaging with spiritual practices brings about a strong sense of well-being. They offer a refuge from the chaos, fostering emotional stability and balance. The peace derived from spiritual engagement isn't just momentary; it weaves its way into the fabric of your life, influencing how you perceive and respond to challenges. This stability can lead to a greater sense of belonging, where you feel part of something larger than yourself. Whether it's a community of like-minded individuals or a deep connection with the universe, this belonging nurtures your spirit, providing comfort and strength. Exploring these practices becomes a source of inner peace, offering insights and perspectives that enrich your life.

Spiritual practices invite you to explore the depths of your soul, offering comfort and guidance. They remind you that healing is about addressing wounds and nurturing a connection to the sacred. As you engage with these practices, you cultivate a relationship with yourself and the world rich with meaning and purpose. Spirituality becomes a companion on your path, offering wisdom, peace, and a sense of belonging that enriches every step.

Creating a Holistic Healing Plan

Creating a holistic healing plan is like crafting a personal map to guide you through life's complexities, explicitly designed for you and by you. When embarking on this path, reflect on your individual goals and values. What are the things that truly matter to you? What do you want to achieve, both physically and emotionally? These reflections help shape your healing plan, ensuring it aligns with your unique needs and aspirations. Ponder on your health and emotions, which are crucial in determining the practices that best support your journey. Whether you are dealing with stress, chronic pain, or emotional challenges, acknowledging these factors is vital. This personalized approach ensures your plan is effective and sustainable, adapting to your evolving needs.

Developing a comprehensive healing plan involves setting achievable goals as stepping stones toward your broader aspirations. Start by identifying small, manageable objectives that can be integrated into your daily routine. These goals include practicing gratitude daily or committing to a weekly yoga class. The key is to balance ambition and practicality, allowing you to celebrate progress without feeling overwhelmed. Integrating mind, body, and soul practices is another essential aspect of a holistic plan. This might involve combining physical activities like walking or dance with spiritual practices such as meditation or journaling. By weaving together these elements, you create a tapestry of healing that nurtures every aspect of your being.

The benefits of a holistic healing plan are significant, enhancing the effectiveness of your journey toward well-being. A comprehensive approach fosters balanced emotional and physical health, making you feel more grounded and resilient. You cultivate a sense of harmony that supports sustained personal growth by addressing multiple facets of your life, from diet to emotional expression. Knowing you have a robust support system, this interconnectedness empowers you to navigate life's challenges confidently. As you progress, your capacity for joy, peace, and fulfillment expands, enriching your relationships and experiences.

Staying committed to your healing plan requires regular self-assessment and reflection. Take time to evaluate your progress and adjust your practices as needed. This might involve journaling about your experiences, noting what works well and where you face challenges. Flexibility is critical, as life is dynamic and ever-changing. Be open to modifying your plan to accommodate new insights or circumstances. You may discover that certain practices no longer resonate with you, or new interests have emerged. Embrace these shifts, as they are natural parts of your growth. Maintaining a holistic healing plan is not about rigid adherence to a set routine but about nurturing a flexible, responsive approach that evolves with you.

By crafting a personalized healing plan, you empower yourself to take charge of your well-being. This plan becomes a living document, guiding you toward a life of balance and fulfillment. It invites you to explore the depths of your being with intentionality and compassion, creating a space where healing can flourish. As you continue this journey, remember that you are not alone. The practices and insights you cultivate along the way provide a foundation of support, connecting you to a community of like-minded individuals who share your commitment to growth and healing. This chapter has offered tools to support your healing journey, bridging the mind, body, and soul. As you look ahead, remember that this plan is your compass, guiding you toward a life of balance and fulfillment. In the next chapter, we'll explore how to sustain this momentum, ensuring your journey unfolds purposefully and joyfully.

Chapter Eight

THRIVING ON YOUR HEALING JOURNEY

"Your healing journey is your greatest adventure." Renee Trudeau

Have you ever looked in the mirror at your reflection and the layers of your life story? It's a powerful moment when you realize that self-discovery is not a destination but a continuous journey, a path of uncovering who you are at every stage of life. This journey is vital because it allows us to grow beyond the scripts written by our past, evolving with each chapter of our lives. Self-discovery is a lifelong endeavor crucial for personal growth and transformation. As we step into new roles and face different challenges, our self-awareness must grow alongside us, adapting to the shifting landscapes of our lives.

Evolving self-awareness is like an artist refining their craft, continuously honing skills, and enhancing understanding. It's about recognizing the nuances of your thoughts, emotions, and reactions. This awareness enables you to navigate life's complexities with greater ease and resilience. As you become more attuned to your inner world, you gain the ability to respond thoughtfully rather than react impulsively. This ongoing process of self-discovery fosters a deeper connection with yourself, empowering you to make choices that align with your values and aspirations. Life is an ever-changing tapestry, and adapting to these changes is essential for growth. By embracing self-discovery, you equip yourself with the tools to thrive amid life's uncertainties.

To embark on this journey of self-exploration, take into account regular self-reflection practices. Set aside time each day to delve into your thoughts and emotions. Keep journaling, as it provides a space for introspection and clarity. Write about your experiences, fears, and dreams, allowing your words to guide you toward a more profound understanding. Engaging in new experiences is another avenue for self-discovery. Step outside your comfort zone and explore activities challenging your perspectives and assumptions. These experiences can reveal hidden aspects of yourself, shedding light on untapped potential and passions. Opening yourself to new possibilities expands your horizons and enriches your self-awareness.

The benefits of perpetual self-discovery are significant, offering a wellspring of personal development and growth. As you continuously explore and understand yourself, you gain greater self-understanding. This self-awareness enhances your ability to make informed decisions, fostering a sense of empowerment and agency. It also enhances adaptability, allowing you to navigate life's transitions gracefully and confidently. When you embrace the journey of self-discovery, you cultivate a mindset of curiosity and openness, inviting new opportunities and experiences into your life. This mindset nurtures resilience, enabling you to bounce back from setbacks and embrace change positively. Through self-discovery, you embark on a path of lifelong learning, continually evolving into the person you were meant to be.

Throughout different life stages, self-discovery takes on various forms and shapes. In midlife, it might manifest as a career change, a shift toward pursuing passions that align with your values. This phase often prompts reflection on past choices and future aspirations, leading to a deeper understanding of your true self. Retirement offers another opportunity for self-discovery as you transition from the structured demands of work to a more open and flexible lifestyle. This stage allows reflection on life's journey, offering a chance to explore new interests and redefine your purpose. Each phase of life presents unique challenges and opportunities for self-discovery, inviting you to embrace change and growth with an open heart. By engaging in self-discovery throughout your life, you cultivate a rich tapestry of experiences and insights, creating a legacy of authenticity and fulfillment.

Reflective Exercise: Journaling for Self-Discovery

Objective: Cultivate ongoing self-awareness and understanding through regular writing practices.

Instructions:

1. **Daily Reflection:** Spend 10 minutes each evening reflecting on your day. Consider what brought you joy, what challenged you, and what you learned about yourself.

2. **Weekly Review:** At the end of each week, review your entries. Identify patterns, themes, or recurring emotions. What do

these reveal about your current state of mind or your personal growth?

3. **Monthly Insight:** Once a month, summarize your reflections. Highlight key insights or revelations. How have you grown or changed? What new understandings have emerged?

Use this practice as a tool for self-exploration, allowing your reflections to guide you toward deeper self-awareness and personal growth.

Building a Supportive Community

Picture a circle of friends who truly understand your struggles and triumphs, a network that uplifts you through every challenge and celebrates each victory. This is the essence of a supportive community, an invaluable asset on your healing journey. A group of people offering emotional support and encouragement can make all the difference. When surrounded by those who share similar experiences, you find comfort in knowing you're not alone. Their stories resonate with yours, creating a tapestry of shared learning and growth. This community acts as a mirror, reflecting the strength and courage you may not see in yourself. In these connections, you discover the power of collective healing, where empathy and understanding lay the groundwork for resilience.

To cultivate such a network, take practical steps to build and nurture connections that support your healing. Start by joining support groups, either in person or online, that align with your needs and interests. These groups provide a safe space to share your journey and learn from others who have walked similar paths. Participating in community activities can also open doors to new friendships and connections. Engaging with others in communal settings fosters a sense of belonging, whether it's a local workshop, a volunteering opportunity, or a book club. Online forums and social media communities offer additional avenues to connect, allowing you to reach beyond geographic boundaries and tap into a global support network. These platforms provide a wealth of resources, from personal stories to expert advice, enriching your journey with diverse perspectives.

The benefits of a strong community extend far beyond emotional support. By surrounding yourself with a network of compassionate individuals, you cultivate an increased sense of belonging, a feeling that you are part of something larger than yourself. This connection fosters a sense of security, enabling you to face life's challenges more confidently. Moreover, community support grants you access to many perspectives and insights. Each person brings unique experiences and wisdom, offering new ways of looking at old problems. As you engage with these diverse viewpoints, you expand your understanding and enhance your adaptability, equipping yourself with the tools to navigate life's complexities gracefully.

Reflect on the story of Sarah, who found solace in a women's support group after a difficult divorce. The group became her lifeline, offering a haven where she could voice her fears and doubts without judgment. Through shared experiences and mutual encouragement, Sarah discovered her inner strength and resilience. This sense of community empowered her to rebuild her life, fostering new friendships and igniting a passion for helping others. Her story is a testament to the transformative power of a supportive network. Similarly, community-driven initiatives, such as neighborhood wellness programs or peer-led workshops, offer opportunities for connection and growth. These initiatives unite people with a common purpose, creating a ripple effect of positive change that extends beyond the individual.

The possibilities for cultivating a supportive community are vast in today's digital landscape. Social media and online forums have transformed our ability to connect, erasing distance and time limitations. You can easily find others who resonate with your journey and aspirations through platforms like Facebook, Reddit, and various wellness apps. These digital spaces offer immediate support and a sense of belonging, ensuring you're never truly alone. In fostering these connections, you nurture a community grounded in mutual support and collective growth. Cherish these bonds, as each interaction enriches your resilience and well-being.

Long-Term Strategies for Emotional Resilience

Emotional resilience is your ability to weather life's storms and emerge stronger on the other side. It's not about avoiding adversity but learning to bounce back from it. This resilience helps you maintain emotional balance, even when things get tough. When you cultivate emotional resilience, you create a foundation of strength that supports your well-being over time. Life is unpredictable and filled with ups and downs, but resilience equips you with the tools to navigate these challenges with grace and determination. It's like having a buoy in turbulent seas, helping you stay afloat and find your way back to calm waters.

Building resilience requires intentional practice and dedication. One powerful approach is developing a growth mindset. This mindset encourages you to view challenges as opportunities for learning and growth rather than insurmountable obstacles. When faced with setbacks, ask yourself what lessons can be gleaned and how to apply them moving forward. It's about shifting your perspective and seeing possibilities where others might see roadblocks.

Practicing gratitude regularly is another effective strategy. By acknowledging the positives in your life, even amid difficult times, you train your mind to focus on abundance rather than scarcity. This practice fosters a sense of contentment and optimism, enhancing your resilience. Stress-reduction techniques, such as mindfulness meditation or deep breathing exercises, support emotional balance. These practices ground you in the present moment, quieting racing thoughts and calming the nervous system. They offer a sanctuary of peace, allowing you to recharge and face challenges with renewed vigor.

The benefits of emotional resilience extend beyond mere survival; they contribute to a fulfilling and balanced life. With improved coping skills, you become adept at handling stress and adversity. You develop the ability to manage emotions constructively, preventing them from overwhelming you. This emotional stability fosters greater life satisfaction as you confidently navigate twists and turns. Resilience empowers you to pursue goals with determination, knowing that setbacks are stepping stones rather than roadblocks. It enhances your relationships as you communicate effectively and empathize with others' struggles. Ultimately, resilience enriches your life, allowing you to thrive in adversity.

This is the story of Emma, a woman who faced tremendous challenges after losing her job unexpectedly. Initially, she felt overwhelmed and uncertain, questioning her self-worth and future. However, Emma embraced a growth mindset, viewing the situation as an opportunity for reinvention. She pursued a new career path aligned with her passions, leveraging her skills in innovative ways. Through gratitude practices, she found solace in the support of loved ones and the small joys in her daily life. Emma's resilience enabled her to navigate and flourish beyond this challenging period. Her story is a testament to the transformative power of resilience. Similarly, stories abound of individuals who have overcome personal adversities—health struggles, financial setbacks, or relationship challenges—by cultivating resilience. These narratives inspire us to see resilience as a dynamic force, propelling us toward growth and fulfillment.

In cultivating emotional resilience, you embark on a lifelong path of strength and adaptability. It's about nurturing your inner resources, knowing you can navigate whatever comes your way. Just as a tree bends with the wind but remains rooted, you can remain steadfast amid life's challenges. With each experience, you deepen your resilience, creating a strength reservoir supporting your well-being. Remember, resilience is not about avoiding difficulties but embracing them as opportunities for growth. It's about trusting yourself and your ability to rise, time and time again.

Embracing Change: Adaptability in Healing

Suppose you're standing at the edge of a vast ocean, waves lapping at your feet, each one different from the last. This is what life often feels like—a constant ebb and flow of change. Adaptability is like learning to dance with the waves rather than resisting them. Adaptability in healing is crucial because it allows us to navigate life's inevitable changes with grace and resilience. As life shifts, so must we. Flexibility in responding to these shifts is essential for sustained growth. Whether it's a change in career, relationships, or personal beliefs, embracing adaptability means being open to the new experiences and lessons life offers. It means understanding that healing is not a linear path but a dynamic process that requires us to adjust our sails in response to the winds of change.

To cultivate adaptability, we can begin by practicing mindfulness and presence. Mindfulness roots us in the present moment, helping us overcome preconceived notions about how things should be. We become more accepting of change by focusing on the here and now. Embracing uncertainty and impermanence is another way to foster adaptability. Instead of fearing the unknown, try to see it as an opportunity for growth. Life is full of surprises, and by accepting that nothing is permanent, we free ourselves from the need to control every outcome. Setting flexible goals also plays a role in developing adaptability. Rather than rigidly clinging to a specific plan, allow room for adjustments. This flexibility encourages you to explore different paths and discover new possibilities.

The benefits of embracing change are far-reaching. As you become more adaptable, your problem-solving skills improve. You learn to approach challenges with creativity and an open mind, finding solutions that may have previously eluded you. Adaptability reduces stress and anxiety; you no longer feel pressured to force situations into a predetermined mold. Instead, you flow with the current, trusting in your ability to navigate whatever comes your way. This mindset fosters resilience as you build confidence to handle life's unpredictability. Every change becomes an opportunity for growth, deepening your understanding of yourself and the world around you.

Ponder the story of Lisa, who found herself at a crossroads after a significant career change. Initially, she felt lost and uncertain, questioning her place in the world. However, rather than resisting the change, Lisa chose to embrace it. She explored new interests and discovered a passion for teaching. This shift led her to a fulfilling career in education, where she thrived by adapting her skills to a new environment. Her reinvention didn't stop there. As she embraced her evolving identity, Lisa found strength and joy in unexpected places, transforming what once felt like a setback into a stepping stone for personal growth. Her journey exemplifies the power of adaptability, showing us that by embracing change, we open ourselves to a world of possibilities.

Embracing change is more than simply accepting the inevitable; it is actively engaging with it. It's about recognizing that change is a constant companion that invites us to expand and evolve. By cultivating adaptability, we equip ourselves with the tools to navigate life's complexities confidently and gracefully. As you embrace change, remember that you are not alone. Countless individuals have walked this path before you, finding strength and resilience in uncertainty. Their stories remind us that adaptability is not just a skill but a way of being—one that enriches our lives and empowers us to thrive, no matter the challenges.

Crafting Your Legacy: Inspiring Others Through Your Healing Journey

Think of your healing story as a beacon, lighting the way for others who tread similar paths. Crafting a legacy through healing is about more than personal transformation; it's about inspiring and impacting others through the authenticity of your journey. Sharing your personal stories allows others to relate, understand, and feel less alone. *Every* experience and *every* insight gained becomes a tool for leading by example. Your vulnerability in sharing highlights your courage and creates a bridge for others to walk alongside you, learning from the trials and triumphs you've faced. This legacy is not built in isolation; it's crafted through the connections you foster and the lives you touch.

There are many ways to share your healing journey, each offering a unique platform to inspire others. Writing or speaking about your experiences can provide meaningful insights and motivation. Whether through a blog, a memoir, or public speaking engagements, your words have the power to reach those who need them most. Mentoring others navigating similar challenges can create a ripple effect of positive change. By guiding someone through their healing, you reinforce your lessons and contribute to a cycle of growth and support. Engaging in community service is another impactful way to share your journey. By working with organizations that align with your healing values, you contribute your time and experience, furthering causes that resonate with your sto ry.

Crafting a legacy through sharing your journey brings immense personal fulfillment and significantly impacts the community. As you inspire others, you create positive change that extends far beyond your immediate circle. Your story becomes a source of hope and strength, encouraging others to embark on their healing paths. This sense of purpose and contribution enhances your life and enriches the lives of those you touch. By crafting your legacy, you build a sense of belonging and connection, knowing that your journey has meaning and significance beyond your healing. It becomes a testament to the resilience of the human spirit, a legacy that continues to inspire long after the initial steps were taken.

In the realm of healing, countless examples of individuals have inspired others through their journeys. Consider the impact of figures like Brené Brown, whose work on vulnerability and shame has transformed how we view emotional health. Her willingness to share her struggles has empowered countless others to embrace their imperfections and find strength in authenticity. Personal testimonials further illustrate the power of a shared legacy. Take the story of Jane, a survivor of domestic violence who now mentors women in similar situations. Her journey from victim to advocate has inspired many to reclaim their power and rebuild their lives. These stories remind us that our experiences, though personal, can have a universal resonance, touching lives in ways we may never fully realize.

As you reflect on crafting your legacy, remember that it is not about perfection but authenticity. It's about sharing the raw, unfiltered version of your journey, the highs and lows, the setbacks and breakthroughs. It's about understanding that your story has the power to inspire, to heal, and to create change. Each step you take in healing contributes to this legacy, shaping a unique narrative. Embrace the opportunity to inspire others through your journey, knowing that your legacy is a living testament to the transformative power of healing. Through your courage and vulnerability, you pave the way for others to find their strength and voice, creating a legacy that resonates far and wide.

In the tapestry of life, your legacy is a thread that weaves through the stories of others, connecting and uplifting. As you continue to craft your legacy, remember that it is a journey of exploration and discovery that evolves with each chapter of your life. Embrace the power of your story and its impact, knowing that your healing journey is a gift to yourself and the world around you. Your legacy, crafted with love and courage, will continue to inspire and empower, leaving an indelible mark on the hearts of those you touch.

BECOMING A BEACON OF HOPE TO OTHERS

Now that you have everything you need to heal your inner child, it's time to share your journey and help others find the same healing path.

By leaving your honest opinion of this book on Amazon, you'll help other women find the support they need and share your passion for inner healing.

Thank you for your help. The journey of healing our inner child continues when we share our knowledge and you're helping me keep this vital work alive.

https://www.amazon.com/review/review-your-purchases/?asin=B0DRZZBCCW

With unconditional love,

Michelle Duffy

CONCLUSION

As we reach the end of this journey together, I invite you to reflect on the transformative power of healing your inner child. This book aims to guide you toward understanding and nurturing those tender parts of yourself. Embracing this journey allows you to foster self-love, break free from negative cycles, and build healthier relationships. Moving away from narratives of guilt and shame, you can step into a space of empowerment and understanding.

Throughout these pages, we've explored childhood experiences' extensive impact on our adult lives. We've delved into how these early encounters shape our emotions, behaviors, and relationships. Key insights have illuminated how reconnecting with your inner child can unlock a reservoir of compassion and resilience. Acknowledging your past creates a foundation for healing and growth, allowing you to respond to life's challenges with greater wisdom and grace.

You've learned practical tools and techniques to help you on this path. Visualization exercises, cognitive behavioral strategies, and mindfulness practices offer ways to nurture and heal your inner child. These tools are not merely theoretical; they are meant to be woven into the fabric of your daily life. The exercises and reflections serve as anchors, guiding you back to your center whenever you feel adrift.

Please take these insights and actively apply them. Use the exercises to explore your emotions and triggers. Work through the journaling prompts to uncover patterns and narratives that no longer serve you. Allow yourself to be vulnerable and open to the healing process, knowing that each step forward is a step toward living a life aligned with your true self.

Think about the ripple effect of your transformation. As you heal, you contribute positively to your relationships, family, and community. Your newfound awareness and compassion can inspire others to embark on their journeys of healing and growth. By modeling empathy and understanding, you create an environment where healthy relationships can flourish.

I want to express my gratitude for embarking on this journey with me. Your willingness to engage with this book reflects your courage and commitment to personal growth. Walking alongside you as you explore the depths of your inner world is an honor. Your dedication to healing is a testament to your strength and resilience.

I envision a future where you continue embracing self-discovery's beauty. This journey doesn't end here. It's a lifelong path that invites you to keep learning and evolving. I hope you move forward with hope and confidence, knowing you have the tools and insights to navigate challenges.

In closing, remember that healing is a journey, not a destination. It's about progress, not perfection. Be gentle with yourself as you continue exploring your inner child's layers. With each step, you are creating a more vibrant and authentic life. You are not alone in this journey; you are part of a larger tapestry of individuals seeking healing and growth. We can create a world filled with compassion, understanding, and love.

Thank you for allowing me to be a part of your journey. May you find peace, joy, and fulfillment as you embrace your inner child and step boldly into the future.

REFERENCES

Brown, M. H. (2024, March 11). Overcoming self-sabotage: Transforming the inner narrative. *Medium*.

Forgiveness: Your health depends on it. (2024, June 20). Johns Hopkins Medicine.

Generational Trauma: Breaking the Cycle of Adverse Childhood Experiences. (2020, December 10). Indiana University Health.

Gordon, S. (2023, August 22). *Somatic therapy may help you deal with past trauma—Here's how*. Health.

Gray, J. (2018, November 18). *15 specific practices to boost self-trust*. Jordan Gray Consulting.

Haslem, H. (2022, December 1). Trauma: The need for a holistic perspective. *CASAT OnDemand*.

Henriques, M. (2019, March 26). *Can the legacy of trauma be passed down the generations?* BBC.

Holzmann, M. (2024, July 18). *The complete guide for using somatic therapy for trauma*. Somatic Therapy Partners.

Horton, A. P. (2019, November 11). *5 Mindfulness Techniques for letting go of control*. Fast Company.

Inner child work: How to heal by reparenting yourself. (n.d.). Big Self School.

Jones, D. (2023, June 6). *Mindful parenting: Building empathy at all ages*. The Tattooed Buddha.

Lachmann, S. (2017, April 10). *When trauma affects your trust in your relationship | psychology today*. Psychology Today.

Lewis, L. (2014). *Navigating the unique challenges of online teaching:(563842014-001)* [Dataset].

Lovering, N. (2016, January 20). *Neuroplasticity and childhood trauma: Effects, healing, and EMDR*. Psych Central.

Migala, J. (2024, August 7). *8 vagus nerve stimulation exercises that help you relax*. Parsley Health.

Neff, Dr. K. (n.d.). Self-Compassion. *Self-Compassion*.

Newport Institute Staff. (2023, May 9). Recovery from trauma and the mind-body connection. *Newport Institute*.

Newport Institute. (2022, July 5). The mind-body connection: What it is & how it impacts mental health. Newport Institute.

Norman, J. (2023, June 29). Inner child healing: Reclaiming joy and wholeness. *The Human Beauty Movement*.

Owen, K. (2023, November 30). *The science of generational patterns: From trauma to transformation*. Jai Institute of Parenting.

Raypole, C. (2021, July 9). The roles neuroplasticity and EMDR play in healing from childhood trauma. PsychCentral.

Rebuilding trust: The power of therapy for betrayal trauma. (2023, September 12). Introspection Counseling Center.

Schore, A. N. (2017). All our sons: The developmental neurobiology and neuroendocrinology of boys at risk. *Infant Mental Health Journal*, *38*(1), 15–52.

Selhub, E. (2015, November 16). *Nutritional psychiatry: Your brain on food*. Harvard Health.

Stoddard, C. (2022, February 22). *Inner child work: What it is, what happened, and how to start healing. Big Self School.*

The long-term effects of childhood trauma on adult relationships: A Jungian perspective - transformative effects | counseling services. (2023, January 22). *Transformative Effects Blog.*

Yalom, V., & Yalom, M.-H. (n.d.). *Peter Levine on trauma healing: A somatic approach.* Pscyhotherapy.Net.

Yuki Miyagawa & Junichi Taniguchi. (2020, December 26). *Self-compassion helps people forgive transgressors: Cognitive pathways of interpersonal transgressions.* Self-Compassion.org. *Psychotherapy.net. (n.d.). Interview with Peter Levine, PhD.*

Van der Horst, D. (2021, October 13). *How to heal your inner child: 8 worksheets and techniques. PositivePsychology.com.*

Van der Horst, D. (2021, October 13). *How to heal your inner child: 8 worksheets and techniques. PositivePsychology.com.*

Leen-Feldner, E. W., Feldner, M. T., Knapp, A., & Bunaciu, L. (2013). *The intergenerational transmission of trauma: Integrating biological and environmental contributions to maternal trauma and child adjustment. Clinical Child and Family Psychology Review, 16(3), 249-264.*

Raypole, C., Capaldo, G., & Lewis, S. L. (2021). *Childhood adversity, attachment, and psychophysiological responses to stress in adulthood. Frontiers in Psychology, 12, 693572.*

ABOUT THE AUTHOR

Michelle Duffy is an author, coach, and transformational teacher who empowers women by guiding them to embrace unconditional love through metaphysical principles, subconscious mind rewiring, and somatic healing. With a B.S. in Industrial Engineering and an MBA from Rice University, Michelle's journey took a transformative turn following a near-death experience. This life-changing event ignited her passion for helping others leading her to pursue postgraduate training in Neuro-linguistic Programming, Hypnotherapy, Transformational Breathwork, Yoga, and Meditation. She has since developed a unique method that blends science and spirituality, focused on releasing trauma and expanding consciousness at mind, body, and soul levels.

Michelle is committed to supporting women in regulating their nervous system and nurturing intentional, fulfilling relationships, especially with their children.

You can connect with her on:

https://www.michelleduffy1111.com

Also by Michelle Duffy

The 10-Minute Meditation Guide for Busy Professionals: An easy and effective way to reduce stress, improve sleep, and have laser-sharp focus.

www.ingramcontent.com/pod-product-compliance
Lightning Source LLC
Chambersburg PA
CBHW061804120626
46550CB00005B/2134